D1583439

Pam Ayres

On Animals

Pam Ayres

On Animals

Illustrated by Ellie Snowdon

EBURY
SPOTLIGHT

2

Ebury Press, an imprint of Ebury Publishing
20 Vauxhall Bridge Road
London SW1V 2SA

Ebury Press is part of the Penguin Random House group of companies whose
addresses can be found at global.penguinrandomhouse.com

Copyright © Pam Ayres 2021

'Walking to Falkirk' and 'Unfed Calf' © Pam Ayres 2006. Reprinted by
permission of Hodder & Stoughton. Originally published in *Surgically
Enhanced* in 2006.

Illustrations © Ellie Snowdon 2021

Design by Julyan Bayes

Pam Ayres has asserted her right to be identified as the author of this Work in
accordance with the Copyright, Designs and Patents Act 1988

First published by Ebury Press in 2021

www.penguin.co.uk

A CIP catalogue record for this book is available from the British Library

ISBN 9781529104967
Printed and bound in Great Britain by Bell and Bain Ltd, Glasgow
Imported into the EEA by Penguin Random House Ireland, Morrison
Chambers, 32 Nassau Street, Dublin D02 YH68.

To my five brilliant grandchildren, and to everyone who loves animals and believes they have a right to their share of the world.

Contents

Introduction

When I was little, my mother had a friend called Mrs Howse and I liked her very much. She lived down the lane from us, and her husband ran a nursery of the horticultural, not the childcare, sort. I would have been about three years old when I was introduced to her dog, a large friendly golden Labrador. This was my first proper encounter with a dog and I was enchanted. Mrs Howse, seeing my sparkle-eyed delight, asked if I would like to give her dog a digestive biscuit. This was a dilemma indeed, because biscuits were a rare sight in our house and if they appeared at all they tended to be of the misleadingly named 'Nice' variety. Fighting down the overwhelming desire to eat the digestive biscuit myself, I heroically fed it to the dog. This is the first time I remember having anything to do with an animal.

The second time, soon after the positive encounter with Mrs Howse's Labrador and now much emboldened, I approached a small Skye terrier called Bessie who liked to lie and sunbathe on the path running behind our row of council houses. Bessie was black with a little topknot, which I fancy was tied with tartan ribbon, but the years may have prettified Bessie beyond how she actually appeared. She was hairy at any rate. Unwisely, as it turned out, I ventured along the path to the prostrate, sun-warmed dog and extended the hand of friendship to give her a pat and stroke. A snarl erupted from the bowels of the prone Bessie as she sprang to her feet, white teeth bared and top knot rigid with fury. I beat a retreat. Clearly all dogs were not the same.

The third dog I remember from my early childhood was called Whisky and he belonged to Mr Wentworth the butcher. All week Whisky would lie in his driveway peacefully thinking dog thoughts and waiting for offal to be slung in his direction. However, every Saturday he did something different. He got to his feet and made his way to the far end of the village, past the school, past the pub, past the sweetshop and various farms, until he reached our house, and there he sat peacefully on the green, waiting for my four brothers and their friends to gather and go over the fields, rabbiting, as they did every weekend. What mysterious kind of dog calendar Whisky had that informed him it was Saturday we never knew, but there he would be, waiting eagerly on the green for his weekly excitement.

I have always liked to be around animals. I had lots of pets, though looking back on them now makes me cringe at my own ignorance and the lack of knowledge that prevailed at that time. I had a poor, tied-up tortoise from the pet shop in Faringdon, which had baskets of them in the windows, fruitlessly climbing over and over each other in a vain attempt to escape their prison. I can still hear the soul-destroying clatter. At home, in cramped hutches, I kept three rabbits, which were seldom, if ever, given water, even on the hottest days, because the general belief was that 'They gets all the moisture they need from the grass.' Hmmm.

I've seldom been without a dog. Some I bought, but most were rejects from various dogs' homes. I have adored them all, they enhanced my life and that of my children. It's funny but when I look back over my life, the regrets I have are mostly for times when I lost patience with an animal and was rough or unkind.

When I was ten or eleven, a generous family in our village let me ride the pony their daughters had outgrown. I don't know if they ever realised how much that meant to me. With six children and little money in the family, there was no hope of me ever having a pony of my own but that was my dream, as it was for countless other small girls. I absorbed every possible bit of information I could find on the subject and at ten years of age could rattle off the names of all the Points of the Horse and Tackle. Even now, I could point you out a shannon bone or a cantle. For years, before hormones turned my eyes thoughtfully towards The Everly Brothers and Roy Orbison or, in their absence, the leather-clad local boys on their motorbikes, I rode Paddy the pony every weekend through a local wood called Hatford Warren. It had soft, sandy soil and a tall whispering line of Scots Pines to greet you as you came clopping in from the road. Then a cathedral-like stillness settled quietly about you; dappled shade, muffled hoofbeats and the indefinable, life-giving fragrance of a big, breathing wood. Those days were priceless to me. I can conjure them up in an instant, the pink-tinted trunks of conifers receding away into darkness, the casual retreat of rabbits, and the incomparable friendly companionship of riding a horse alone, watching the wood unfold beyond a pair of pricked ears.

I grew up and, at the age of eighteen, joined the WRAF to travel. At nineteen I was in Singapore, where you ran the risk of being bitten by monkeys as you cycled to the swimming pool, and where chameleons changed colour as they moved among the bushes of the garden.

After I married and had children, we had guinea pigs, hens, sheep, cattle and a few athletic goats. I hope they all combined to form part of a happy and interesting childhood.

Some years later we kept animals for meat, but I never got used to that. It made sense to try, as my family were enthusiastic meat-eaters, and I reasoned that I could give our animals a truly good life, making sure they were well cared for and content. Inevitably, though, the animal comes to trust you and I could not cope with the betrayal at the end, just loading them up for the abattoir. People told me that I'd get used to it but they were wrong, I didn't. I was glad when that phase came to an end.

These days I have just one pet dog and I try to help the wildlife that abounded on all sides as I was growing up in rural Berkshire and which, heartbreakingly, has disappeared. The innumerable little water voles which inhabited the brook, the tumbling flocks of lapwings, snuffling hedgehogs, hordes of chirping sparrows dust-bathing on country roads, starlings, swifts and swallows. They are all gone.

I bought a little piece of land as an oasis, a place to plant native trees, shrubs and hedges, just one tiny spot where wildlife could come and find a home. When I see a frog, a hare or a skylark there, and I know they aren't going to be sprayed, hunted or injured by farm machinery in that small safe haven, well, that's a good enough legacy for me. I would have bought more if I could.

Here, in one volume, are all the poems connected with animals that I have written so far. I have arranged them with the oldest starting first, as in some ways they are like a diary. Incredibly, some are now about fifty years old! I have added a few introductions, and an explanation here and there, especially where times and attitudes have changed. I hope you like them. Thank you, as always, for buying my book.

Pam Ayres, 2021

Hens at Home

I have mixed feelings about this poem 'The Battery Hen' now, a combination of gratitude for the process it set in motion and sheepishness about the flippant, mickey-taking tone.

When I wrote it in the early seventies, I knew that battery farms existed and I had glimpsed the louvred ventilators of those long sheds hidden behind tall hedges. I had heard talk about laying hens crammed into small cages, but I didn't know any detail about the boiling hot, stacked-high conditions inside those windowless buildings.

I was born in 1947, two years after the end of WWII. At that frugal time, every family I knew kept laying hens in a run at the bottom of the garden. This practice was part of the desperate need for food self-sufficiency during and immediately after the war, and it was applauded as a way of avoiding waste.

We kept chickens in the garden of our council house in Stanford in the Vale for as long as I can remember and, looking back, they were the ultimate eco-friendly waste disposal system. Any food scraps were flung over the wire netting to the birds, and at bedtime Mum would wedge a great blackened saucepan brimming with the day's vegetable peelings and small 'pig taters' into the dying embers of the fire, to boil up and soften overnight. In the morning, the resulting mush was strained, mashed with layers' meal from the village grain merchants, enriched with a shake of fiery pepper which was supposed to crank up the workings of the laying hen, bludgeoned with a thick stick and fed hot, steaming and fragrant to the waiting hens. One of my four brothers was sent off to the chicken run to give them their breakfast. I can see him now, staggering up the frost-white grass path, wreathed in clouds of steam from the black saucepan. My mother would watch him go with satisfaction. 'That'll warm 'em,' she'd say.

Over time their enclosure would become lifeless, sour, denuded of grass, so Dad would fork it over to expose fresh earth. The ecstatic birds would circle the run at a frantic pace, earthworms dangling from their beaks. Dad would also throw over any spent plants from the allotment and these were welcomed with delight, scratched over, scrutinised for insects and, if they were brassicas, devoured. It was a fair exchange. We regarded them fondly, they were part of the family and certainly the eggs formed an essential part of our daily fare. Our mother used to say, 'You got an egg, you got a meal!'

So that was my experience of laying hens. Big warm eggs and happy birds fluffing up their feathers in dusty dips. I had no real notion of battery hens and their short wretched lives. This changed later when I became involved with the good work of the British Hen Welfare Trust.

I can't remember what prompted me to write 'The Battery Hen'. I think it just came to me and I wrote it down as a bit of fun because I liked poultry and loved writing. Personally, it is a hugely significant piece because it was the first thing I ever read on the radio. Stiff with fear, sometime in 1972 or 3, I went into the recently established BBC Radio Oxford and recited this poem for their poetry spot. When I finished reading it, the producer, Andy Wright, said something to me that I never forgot, words which really did change my life completely.

He said: 'If you've got any more like that, we'll have them.'

BBC Radio Oxford offered me a contract to come up with more humorous poems. I told Andy I was terrified of deadlines because I had no idea if I could write to order. He suggested a period of six months, which I felt comforted by, and I went away incredulous, speechless with joy that something I had written was considered valuable by *the BBC! And they wanted more!* It was one of the happiest days of my life.

The poem was aired, and immediately noticed and featured on the weekly farming programme. Next, an excited voice from BBC Radio Oxford rang to say it had been chosen for BBC Radio 4's *Pick of the Week! Pick of the Week!* A roundup of the *best parts of the whole week's programmes!* Incredibly, it was then picked up by the Canadian Broadcasting Company and aired across Canada! Letters poured through the door of my home in High Street, Witney, asking for copies. It was staggering. So, this simple poem was the beginning, the key that enabled me to spend the next fifty years of my life writing for my living, doing the thing I love best.

The Battery Hen

Oh, I am a battery hen,
On me back there's not a germ,
I never scratched a farmyard,
And I never pecked a worm.
I never had the sunshine,
To warm me feathers through,
Eggs I lay. Every day.
For the likes of you.

Now. When you has them scrambled,
And piled up on your plate,
It's me what you should thank for that,
I never lays them late,
I always lays them reg'lar,
I always lays them right,
I never lays them brown,
I always lays them white.

But it's no life for a battery hen,
In me box I'm sat,
A funnel stuck out from the side,
Me pellets comes down that,
I gets a squirt of water,
Every half a day,
Watchin' with me beady eye,
Me eggs roll away.

I lays them in a funnel,
Strategically placed,
So that I don't kick 'em,
And let them go to waste,
They rolls off down the tubing,
And up the gangway quick,
Sometimes I gets to thinkin',
'That could have been a chick!'

I might have been a farmyard hen,
Scratchin' in the sun,
There might have been a crowd of chicks,
After me to run,
There might have been a cockerel fine,
To pay us his respects,
Instead of sittin' here,
Till someone comes and wrings our necks.

I see the Time and Motion clock,
Is sayin' nearly noon.
I 'spect me squirt of water,
Will come flyin' at me soon,
And then me spray of pellets,
Will nearly break me leg,
And I'll bite the wire nettin',
And lay one more bloody egg.

The Decline of Hedgehogs

'In Defence of Hedgehogs' was another early effort, from about 1971. Around that time, I used to write in the evenings in my rented flat. I loved doing it; my executive desk was an ironing board across the arms of a comfy chair. There was no thought of any of my work being published, I wrote for the joy of it, as an antidote to my job. I was working as a secretary for a company in Witney, and there was nothing in the work that remotely interested me, nothing about the hydraulic kit or air-moving equipment they manufactured that didn't fill me with a deadly, hopeless feeling of being in an environment where I had absolutely nothing to offer. I used to go for a walk at lunchtime down to the picturesquely named village of Crawley, and I dreamed of just carrying on walking, of never having to go back. I despaired of the job, but I didn't know how to break out of it. It paid well enough and the people were nice, but the work made me feel at rock bottom.

In the evenings I set up my ironing board and wrote with a kind of desperation. I never analysed it then but now, looking back, I can see that it was an outlet for the creativity I had that was so suppressed. I was brought up to believe that you got yourself a job, any job that supported you, and if you could paint and draw and write and make things, that was all well and good, but it didn't pay the bills and should be shoved into the background. I never questioned it. Miraculously, and unlike so many other people with similar skills, I found a way to break out and use my abilities to make a career.

When I wrote 'In Defence of Hedgehogs', I was living at home in Stanford in the Vale. Every morning I drove dejectedly to work in my Morris 1000, which I resented because it did not match my aspirations in life. Quite the reverse. I was young, in my twenties, but this was the matronly car of a matronly old biddy; I had purchased it from my brother Allan for fifty quid. It clearly demonstrated how hard up I was, emitting vast, noxious clouds of smoke from the exhaust, and dismally failing to present the driver as a class act. Indeed, people doubled up laughing as I passed.

My route to work took me past the wood called Hatford Warren, where each morning at that early hour a fresh crop of squashed hedgehogs would lie on the road, having been run over the night before. I don't know why they gathered on the road in such numbers instead of staying in the safety of the wood, but they did, and once there, they were run over and left around like black litter. I found this inestimably sad, which doesn't come across in the poem. I don't perform it much now, and indeed I feel a bit guilty about it. I'm delighted that people like it, but there is something about the jolly, jokey tone that grates on me these days.

When I wrote it, the idea that hedgehogs would one day disappear was unthinkable, preposterous. They were everywhere. Today, British hedgehog numbers are so depleted that they are officially listed by the Mammal Society as vulnerable to extinction. In the 1950s the population was estimated to be fifty million, now the figure is one million if we're lucky. How can this have happened?

Most of all, because of the disastrous loss of hedgerows and the rich habitat they provided. The big, impoverished fields that are sprayed out and insect-poor. Careless tossing of slug pellets, fenced-in gardens with no access for foraging hedgehogs, and the busy roads dividing up the countryside so that individuals that do survive cannot mix and cannot breed. The genetic pool of the hedgehog spins ever smaller.

I like hedgehogs. I like them a lot and am patron of our local wildlife hospital, where hundreds of late-born, skinny ones are nursed through the winters and fattened up ready for release in the spring. There has been a gratifying move to take in hedgehogs and repopulate big estates such as Woburn Abbey, Althorp House and Chatsworth, as well as outstanding efforts by farmers, gardeners and people with no land at all. The fight is on to preserve this, our only spiny mammal, and I hope we win.

Because I wrote these poems to perform myself, with my own timing and accent, this appears in a kind of half-baked dialect. It felt important to me to write it as I would have said it, with a sense of fun and plenty of bouncin' and whistlin' and hoverin'. It looks cumbersome to me now, but then, if I wrote the words correctly, they looked formal and wrong. They just didn't sound like me.

In Defence of Hedgehogs

I am very fond of hedgehogs,
Which makes me want to say,
That I am struck with wonder,
How there's any left today,
For each morning as I travel,
And no short distance that,
All I see are hedgehogs,
Squashed. And dead. And flat.

Now, hedgehogs are not clever,
No, hedgehogs are quite dim,
And when he sees your headlamps,
Well, it don't occur to him,
That the very wisest thing to do,
Is up and run away,
No! He curls up in a stupid ball,
And no doubt starts to pray.

Well, motor cars do travel,
At a most alarming rate,
And by the time you sees him,
It is very much too late,
And thus he gets a-squasho'd,
Unrecorded but for me,
With me pen and paper,
Sittin' in a tree.

It is statistically proven,
In chapter and in verse,
That in a car-and-hedgehog fight,
The hedgehog comes off worse.
When whistlin' down your prop shaft,
And bouncin' off your diff,
His coat of nice brown prickles,
Is not effect-iff.

A hedgehog cannot make you laugh,
Whistle, dance or sing,
And he ain't much to look at,
And he don't make anything,
And in amongst his prickles,
There's fleas and bugs and that,
But there ain't no need to leave him,
Squashed. And dead. And flat.

Oh, spare a thought for hedgehogs,
Spare a thought for me,
Spare a thought for hedgehogs,
As you drink your cup of tea,
Spare a thought for hedgehogs,
Hoverin' on the brinkt,
Spare a thought for hedgehogs,
Lest they become extinct.

The Frogmarch

This is a tale about frogs, which every spring heroically journey back to the pond in which they were hatched in order to meet other frogs and breed. To these small creatures, motorways are a major, lethal obstacle.

You might not understand the reference to St Giles' Fair. Founded in 1625, this is a massive fair that takes place over two days in the centre of Oxford. It arrives in the city loaded on an endless succession of lorries, trailers and associated caravans, so if you were a frog waiting to cross the road as it passed, you would have to wait a very, very long time …

Move along the kerbstone there,
And get back into line,
I know we've all been sitting here,
Since twenty-five past nine,
Based on my traffic census,
And with no more hesitation,
I reckon by tonight,
We'll reach the central reservation.

Now, I don't want my tactics,
Criticised again today,
I realise that everybody,
Knew a better way,
But you are simple country folk,
You do not often come,
In contact with these heavy lorries,
Rattling down to Brum.

I know that when compared,
To boggy riverbanks and peat,
This M40 motorway,
Is murder on your feet,
I also know that in the usual
Places where we sit,
We don't arise to find
Our underneath stuck up with grit.

Life for us amphibians,
Is getting very harsh,
Take the Witney by-pass,
That used to be a marsh,
They've irrigated all the land,
It's all gone to the dogs,
You get fantastic drainage,
But you don't get any frogs.

Still, keep your wits about you, lads,
Before we are much older,
We'll all be in the Promised Land,
And off of this hard shoulder,
All the female frogs are there,
Waiting in the bower,
Famed for their attractiveness,
That Sutton Coldfield shower.

Right then, watch the traffic,
Now I think I see a gap!
Wake that sleeping beauty up,
His head sunk in his lap,
Get your bits and pieces then,
Is everybody there?
Look left! … Prepare to spring!
Oh, NO! Here comes St Giles' Fair!

I'm a Starling ... Me Darling

Our mother was a very kind person who always encouraged us to respect and care for animals. We especially enjoyed feeding wild birds, and from her commentary I effortlessly learned all their names. My Uncle Sam worked on the railways and made us a bird table out of railway sleepers. It was sturdy. If a pterodactyl had flapped down and roosted on it, it wouldn't have flinched.

You couldn't buy designated bird food then, so we offered anything we thought they might like: half a coconut won at the fair, peanuts in their shells threaded on to strings, tied-up bundles of bacon rind, crumbled bread, cake or dollops of dripping. Having laid out the feast, we would rush indoors and wait behind the curtain to see what came. We hoped to see the beautiful native birds – the blackbird with his golden beak, a marvellous speckled thrush, dear little blue tits, shy wrens with their sticking-up tails, pink chaffinches or a vibrant, red-breasted robin. And see them we did, in a wondrous parade as we watched, stock-still and holding our breath, behind the curtain. It was magical but short lived.

Soon one starling would arrive and swagger round the banquet. Then another. To groans from the spectators, the sky turned black. A vast multitude of starlings would descend on the food like a plague of locusts and scoff the lot. Our bird table was picked clean. The birdwatching was declared over, it was time to find something else to do. We all trudged dejectedly off.

Nobody liked starlings then. There were so many of them, great voracious mobs, confident and greedy. None of us thought for a moment that those enormous flocks which filled the evening sky would diminish in the way they have, or that they would ever be on the red list of endangered species as they are today.

*

We're starlings, the missis, meself and the boys,
We don't go round hoppin', we walks,
We don't go in for this singing all day,
And twittering about, we just squawks.

We don't go in for these fashionable clothes,
Like old Mistle Thrush and his spots,
Me breast isn't red, there's no crest on me head,
We've got sort of, hardwearing … dots.

We starlings, the missis, meself and the boys,
We'll eat anything that's about,
Well, anything but the half coconut,
I can't hold it still. I falls out.

What we'd rather do is wait here for you,
To put out some bread for the tits,
And then, when we're certain you're there by the curtain,
We flocks down and tears it to bits.

But we starlings, the missis, meself and the boys,
We reckon that we're being got at,
You think for two minutes, them finches and linnets,
You never sees them being shot at.

So the next time you comes out, to sprinkle the crumbs out,
And there's starlings there, making a noise,
Don't you be so quick, to heave half a brick,
It's the missis, meself and the boys!

The Hegg

It wasn't until 1967 that the contraceptive pill became readily available to all. Previously it had only been prescribed to married women. I wrote this at a time when pregnancy outside marriage was still seriously shameful, and the dubious skills of backstreet abortionists were still being sought.

It's quite a jolly jape, but the underlying theme wasn't so funny.

A thrush, disconsolate, with no sign of a mate,
Sat morbidly perched in a tree,
Saying, 'I tell the tale,
Of a flighty young male,
Who have done the dirty on me.

'I'm Hexpecting a Hegg, a Hillicit Hegg,
A Hegg lyeth here, in my breast,
While the trees were bright-leaved,
I rashly conceived,
A Hegg, Houtside of the Nest.

'For my deed I am shunned, and left moribund,
And by all I am left on a limb,
I would give my right wing,
To be rid of this thing,
And for my great girth to be slim.'

Just then a black crow, with his black eyes a-glow,
Boldly down to the thrush flew,
Said, 'The grapevine, I've heard,
Tells of a distressed bird,
Which I've reason to think may be you.'

He stood on one leg, said, 'You're having an Egg,
And the other birds feel you are bad,
But if with me you came,
You'd be free of the shame,
Of having an egg with no dad.

'For a nominal fee, I will take you to see,
My friend, who lives up the back doubles,
If you swear not to fail,
To pay on the nail,
He will duff up the source of your troubles!'

So the thrush, unafraid, assented and paid,
And went under cover of night,
To see an old Bustard,
With gin and with mustard,
And to be relieved of her plight.

She was made to sit in a bathful of gin,
And she was obliging and meek,
She was made to consume,
Some soap and a prune,
And her feathers fell out for a week.

Outside on the bough, she said, 'Look at me now,
Of my Hegg I am freed, but I'm Hill,
And if Hagain I stray,
Without naming the day,
Then first I shall go on the Pill.'

Pam Ayres and the Embarrassing Experience with the Parrot

We've always lived close to the Cotswold Wildlife Park, a pleasant sort of zoo near Burford in Oxfordshire. One day I visited it with a friend, and this is almost exactly what happened, except that I have slightly embroidered the end. The violence didn't materialise, only the inclination to wield it.

Satisfying ends to the kinds of performance poems I write are tantalising and elusive. They make or break what has gone before and are worth striving to devise. Even if your ode is a work of undiluted genius at the start, if the ending is only a disappointing damp squib, then that is all your audience is left with, a thing that started out well but fell flat and petered out.

I was always pleased with the end of this one for its sense of having come full circle. Also, when performing this on stage, I get the opportunity to portray a half-dead parrot swaying on one leg, which is a great dramatic moment.

'The Battery Hen' was the first poem I ever performed on radio. This was the first one that I, knock-kneed with terror, ever declaimed on television.

At the Cotswold Wildlife Park,
In the merry month of May,
I paid the man the money,
And went in to spend the day,
Straightway to the Pets Corner,
I turned my eager feet,
To go and see the rabbits,
And give them something to eat.

As I approached the hutches,
I was alarmed to see,
A crowd of little yobbos,
Hollering with glee,
I crept up close behind them,
And weighed the scene up quick,
And saw them poke the rabbits,
Poke them! … with a stick!

'Get off you little devils!'
I shouted in their ear,
'Don't you poke them rabbits!
That's not why they are here!'
I must have really scared them,
For in seconds they were gone,
And feeling I had done some good,
I carried on along.

Till up beside the Parrots Cage,
I stood to view the scene,
They were lovely parrots,
Beautiful blue and green,
In and out the nest box,
They were really having fun,
Squawking out and flying about,
All except for one.

One poor old puffed-up parrot,
Clung grimly to his perch,
And as the wind blew frontwards,
Backwards, he would lurch,
One foot up in his feathers,
Abandoned by the rest,
He sat there, plainly dying,
With his head upon his chest.

Well, I walked on down the pathway,
And I stroked a nanny goat,
But the thought of parrots dying,
Brought a lump into my throat,
I could no longer stand it,
And to the office I fled,
Politely I began: 'S'cuse me,
Your parrot's nearly dead.'

Well, me and a curator,
In urgent leaps and bounds,
With a bottle of Parrot Cure,
Dashed across the grounds,
The dust flew up around us,
As we reached the Parrots Pen,
And the curator he turned to me,
Saying, 'Which one is it then?'

You know what I am going to say:
He was not there at all,
At least, not where I left him,
No, he flew from wall to wall,
As brightly as a button,
Did he squawk and jump and leap,
The curator was very kind,
Saying, 'I expect he was asleep.'

But I was humiliated,
As I stood before the wire,
The curator went back,
To put his feet up by the fire,
So I let the parrot settle,
And after a short search,
I found the stick the yobbos had,
And poked him off his perch.

The Stuffed Horse

Faringdon was my home town when I was growing up, but I've always pictured this next drama unfolding in Wantage, which was a couple of miles further away. Perhaps it's because in the Market Square stands a statue of King Alfred the Great, a jolly good egg born in Wantage in 849. At a comfortable height round the base of the statue is a series of steps, ideal for sitting on to enjoy the bustling little town scene, to wait for the bus or drink a cup of tea. This is the plinth upon which I imagine the stuffed horse once stood, as a fine example of the taxidermist's art and these the very steps where the unsuspecting victims were peremptorily coshed.

Now, in 2021, I thought about changing the dated reference to *Fabian of the Yard,* but as it had been a gripping and unmissable television detective series during my childhood, I felt that referring to a modern TV programme wouldn't be right. So, in this story Fabian detects on, and the pound note, for so long defunct, springs crisply back into life.

There was a stuffed horse what had died,
And the townspeople stood it with pride,
On a plinth in the Square,
And the shoppers went there,
And sat, for a rest, by its side.

Beneath the stuffed horse was a plaque,
Only vandals had painted it black,
What told of the deed,
Of the glorious steed,
And the General, what rode on its back.

The bold horse, with never a care,
Had ducked cannonballs in the air,
And stood to the end,
By the General, his friend,
Which was why he was put in the Square.

Well, his tail it was stuck out with wire,
And paint made his nostrils afire,
And his bold eye of glass,
Gazed upon concrete grass,
When he met with his fate, what was dire.

In town, in the criminal quarter,
In buildings with mouldering mortar,
A voice whispered, 'Right,'
And into the night,
Rushed ten men … and one who was shorter.

They lay by the horse with no word,
And the soft sound of sawing was heard,
In silence, all night,
Stuffin' flew left and right,
And into a sack was transferred.

When the church clock struck quarter to four,
Ten men ran away, and a saw,
But the short one, my friend,
Was not there at the end,
He was with his companions no more.

When morning it broke on the Square,
You would never have known they'd been there,
For the horse gazed away,
Like the previous day,
Just sniffin' the spring in the air.

But walkin' across to the spot,
Came two ladies whose feet had grown hot,
They sat on the ground,
And one got out a pound,
Saying: 'Here's that quid I owed to you, Dot.'

From the back of the stuffed horse's throat,
Came a hand and it snatched the pound note!
With the hand, and the cash,
The jaws shut with a clash,
And the horse gazed away with a gloat.

The lady was helped off to bed,
'I thought they liked hay, dear,' she said,
No one listened, of course,
For it was a stuffed horse,
What never required to be fed.

But it happened again, the next day,
When a vicar had sat down to pray,
He said, 'Lord, bless my flock,'
When a great lead-filled sock,
Took his senses, and wallet, away.

But by now the long arm of the law,
Started pickin' up pieces of straw,
What might have been nothin',
But could have been stuffin',
And random observers, they saw:

That the stuffed horse's eye, though of glass,
Had seemed to be watchin' them pass,
And sometimes would blink,
Or give you a wink,
As if to say, 'Step on my grass ...'

Hadrian of the Yard, he was called,
He was like Fabian, only bald,
He suspected a snatcher,
(a man of short stature),
Inside of the horse was installed.

And indeed, that great sleuth, he was right!
By Caesarean, they caught him that night,
Ten men and a saw,
Had broken the law,
Illegal entry, all right.

But tragic indeed was the scene,
In the place where the stuffed horse had been,
Bandy-legged and defaced,
He had to be replaced,
By an ordinary bust,
    of the Queen.

The Vegetable Garden and the Runaway Horse

I wrote this in the very, very early days when the whole idea of me writing 'poetry' was a joke. In the early seventies there were folk clubs in pubs everywhere. People would get together to have a drink and a laugh, and to sing. I adored those clubs; they were a godsend to me. I didn't know anything about singing, but I was mesmerised by people who could really do it, could weave together harmonies that were thrilling to hear. All sorts of travelling singers and musicians were booked and each of them had different styles. It is no exaggeration to say that I lived for Monday nights at the Bell Inn in Ducklington. At work I was a bored secretary, but there I was a somebody, a joker who could sing and play the guitar a bit, and who could usually come up with some daft bit of verse to give everyone a laugh. That was the situation when I wrote this. Soon afterwards I went on television, people started to buy my books in large numbers and then I tried hard to write as well as I could. Here, I'm just mucking about.

In everybody's garden now,
The grass has started growing,
Gardeners, they are gardening,
And mowers … they are mowing,
Compost heaps are rotting down,
And bonfires burning low,
So I took up me shovel,
And resolved to have a go.

I dug a patch of garden,
That was not too hot or shady,
And not too large to tax
The constitution of a lady.
Everything which crossed my spade,
I flung it all asunder,
And that which I could not dig up,
I rapidly dug under.

And in my little plot,
I bravely laboured with the hoe,
Enthusiasm running rife,
I sprinted to and fro,
I stopped for nothing,
Not for food or drink or idle words,
Except a spotted dick,
Someone had chucked out for the birds.

Imagine then my pleasure,
As it all came sprouting out,
I cast aside me dibber,
And I swaggered round about,
But, alas, the gate,
To which my garden was adjacent,
Was open, and I never saw,
As up the path I hastened.

When I went down on Saturday,
A horse stood in my plot,
But nothing else stood in it,
For he'd eaten all the lot,
I said, 'Alas, my efforts wasted,
And my garden wrecked,
Go away, you rotten horse,'
(Or words to that effect).

His hooves had crushed me lettuce,
And me radishes were mangled,
Broken canes were scattered,
Where me runner beans had dangled,
The lovely shiny marrow,
I'd been going to stuff and all,
The horse had broken off its stalk, and kicked it up the wall.

Standing in the ruins,
Of me Brussels sprouts and spinach,
I threw away me shovel,
And I said, 'Well, that's the finich,
No early peas for me,
The birds can have them,
Or the mice might,
And if I want a cabbage,
Well, I'll see you down at Pricerite.'

A Big Mistake

As soon as I started working for myself I bought a black Labrador puppy called Lucy, which was the last thing on earth I should have done. I had always wanted a dog of my own, but I hadn't thought it through, and the experience was nightmarish.

The puppy was the result of an unplanned liaison between two Labradors that happened to live next door to one another. I foolishly bought this appealing little animal for ten quid and took her home in a shoebox. I had some sort of vague image of me with the perfectly trained adult dog, basking in its devotion and fondly watching it obey my every calm command. How I thought I was going to achieve it, I do not know.

Of course, the little creature was lonely and wailed bitterly all night. In desperation, I took her upstairs with me and hung an arm out of bed to fondle her ears every time she cried. Of course, she peed everywhere and fouled the carpet. It was hideous, and I was too obstinate to admit that I'd made a dreadful mistake. As I now had a new job of wandering poet, I had to go away quite a lot. Bored and baffled, she dragged the stuffing out of my new sofa in my new home. She gnawed the legs of my new table. When I took her out, she pulled against the lead with extraordinary strength. It was exhausting; she walked the whole distance on her two back legs. I was at my wits' end.

My dad, Stan, had watched this debacle quietly as it unfolded. He knew how to treat a puppy and, eventually, white with relief, I took her over to my parents' home to live. They took the awful responsibility off my shoulders and gave her a good home. I had made every single mistake in the book and should never have gone within a hundred miles of a dog at that time. I had made no preparations, done no research and had not a clue what to expect. I did at least get this little verse from the harrowing experience, but reading it suggests a lot more light-heartedness than I felt at the time. When I next took on a dog, I made sure the circumstances were better, and that I had a serious amount of time to spend on getting both of us off to a good start.

Puppy Problems

I bought myself a puppy and I hoped in time he might,
Become my friend and ward off things that go bump in the night,
I put him in a shoe box and at home I took him out,
And then began to learn what owning puppies is about.

I tried so hard to love him, and I didn't rave or shout,
When he bit into the sofa and he dragged the stuffing out,
I *gave* him things to chew, but soon I couldn't fail to see,
That he liked the things he found, more than the things supplied
    by me.

He frayed my lovely carpet that I'd saved my money for,
And when he wasn't chewing, he was weeing on the floor,
He didn't spare the table leg, that came in for a gnaw,
I told him, but the message never seemed to reach his jaw.

We laboured at the gardening, me and my little pup,
At two I planted flowers, and at four he dug them up,
He liked to dig, he'd bury bones, and pat them down so neat,
And then he'd rush indoors as clods of mud flew off his feet.

I bought a book on training, and I read it all one night,
And when we set off out, I really thought we'd got it right,
With titbits in my coat to give him once he got the knack,
But he didn't, so I couldn't, so I ate them coming back.

When I commanded 'Heel!' he never seemed to take the point,
But galloped on half-strangled, tugging my arm out of joint,
He jumped up people's clothes, the cleaning bills I had to pay!
And when I shouted 'Here!' he turned and ran the other way.

One day I drove him over, and I gave him to my dad,
Who welcomed him and trained him, but it left me very sad,
So I thought I'd let you know, in case a pup's in store for you,
That it's very wise indeed to have a dad who likes dogs too.

The Bunny Poem

Along with 'Oh, I Wish I'd Looked after Me Teeth' and
'I Am a Drystone Waller', this poem is the one people are
most likely to quote at me when I'm walking down the street.
'Oi Pam,' they say, 'Is that bunny rabbit
still waiting?'

I am a bunny rabbit,
Sitting in me hutch,
I like to sit up this end,
I don't care for that end much.
I'm glad tomorrow's Thursday,
'Cause with a bit of luck,
As far as I remember,
That's the day they pass the buck.

Clive the Fearless Birdman

The first time I visited Melbourne in Australia was in 1978 when the Moomba Festival was at its height. This is a huge, happy, free and famous festival, part of which is a birdman competition staged to raise funds for charity. A flock of birdmen in spectacular plumage flap their unconvincing wings and leap cheerfully off the bridge into the Yarra River to be scooped up by waiting lifeboats, and the scene is absurd, colourful and uproariously funny. I was touring Australia then, and appearing on various TV programmes to publicise my performances. Sometime previously, by great good fortune, I had written 'Clive the Fearless Birdman'. I couldn't tell you why, it was just a daft idea that turned up one day, but there in the middle of the Moomba Festival it was entirely apt. People thought I had written it specially which, shamefully, I did not deny.

There are one or two lines I especially like in my poems. Here, Seth's line, '"If he jumps off the steeple, I shan't have to dig a hole,"' is one of my favourites.

Clive the fearless birdman was convinced that he could fly,
At night he lay in bed and dreamt of soaring through the sky,
Of winging through the clouds, of gliding far out into space,
And he had a leather helmet with a beak stuck on the face.

Clive the fearless birdman had a wife who did not care,
For his fly-by-night ambition of cavorting through the air,
With mockery and ridicule she did her best to kill it,
And cruelly filled his breakfast dish with cuttlefish and millet.

But in his little potting shed he'd built some mighty wings,
From balsa wood and sticky tape and plasticine and strings,
Up to his neck in feathers which had taken months to pluck,
He laboured with his Evo-Stick, he fashioned and he stuck.

He tried it on at last and slowly turned from side to side,
So wonderful was it, that Clive the birdman slumped and cried,
So shiny were the feathers, all in silver grey and black,
With eiderdown all up the front and turkey down the back.

It strapped on with a harness, buckled round his arms and throat,
All made adjustable to fit the thickness of his coat,
Just to see him walking down the street made women shriek,
As he flapped by in his harness, and his helmet and his beak.

So Clive announced to all the culmination of his search,
And he told the local papers he'd be jumping off the church,
Seth, the old gravedigger, with his face as black as coal,
Said 'If he jumps off the steeple, I shan't have to dig a hole.'

And so the day arrived, and all the people came to stare,
Police held back the crowds, and all the local press were there,
Clive read out a noble speech, an address to the people,
That nobody could hear, for it was windy up the steeple.

He stepped out into space and flapped his wings just for a minute,
Far above the vicar's garden, as he plummeted straight in it,
He lay there in the cabbages without another flutter,
And the beak came off his helmet and went rolling in the gutter.

But far away in Heaven, Clive the birdman reigns supreme,
Soaring through the air without the aid of jet or steam,
So at the Pearly Gates, if it's with Clive you wish to speak,
You can tell him by his harness, and his helmet, and his beak.

Clamp the Mighty Limpet

I like the idea of an obstreperous limpet, one that studies you threateningly from under the edge of his shell and thinks warlike thoughts. I used to imagine that they just sat on their rock, year in, year out, and didn't do much. My husband once said I had the brain of a limpet, which I took to be an unusual insult, and one day I happened to mention this on the radio.

In response I received a most comforting letter from a marine biologist who had been listening. He said I should not be at all put out by my husband's comment because, in fact, the limpet is a highly resourceful and admirable critter. Apparently, the limpet moulds himself to one particular spot and waits to be submerged when the tide comes in. Once under water, he releases his suction pad and sets off at a smart pace, scuttling over the rocks on various bits of limpet business. However, and this is the crux of the matter, as soon as the limpet senses that the tide is receding, he can somehow navigate back to his original, exact spot, and there orientate and clamp himself to precisely the same place. Therefore, said the marine biologist, the brain of a limpet was not a thing to be sniffed at, and I should ignore my husband. Which I usually do.

I am Clamp the Mighty Limpet,
I am solid, I am stuck,
I am welded to the rockface,
With my superhuman suck,
I live along the waterline,
And in the dreary caves,
I am Clamp the Mighty Limpet!
I am Ruler of the Waves.

What care I for the shingle,
For the dragging of the tide,
With my unrelenting sucker,
And my granite underside?
There's only one reward,
For those who come to prise at me,
And that's to watch their fingernails,
As they go floating out to sea.

Don't cross me, I'm a limpet,
Though it's plankton I devour,
Be very, very careful,
I can move an inch an hour!
Don't you poke or prod me,
For I warn you – if you do,
You stand there for a fortnight,
And I'll come and stick on you!

The Rat Resuscitation Rhyme

I feel sorry for rats, that they are detested and massacred without a second thought. I know they carry disease and inhabit the foulest of places and no, I wouldn't want them running free in my house, but rats are such tragically *smart* animals. They are intelligent and quick to learn, yet their fate is to be hated, poisoned, trapped, and experimented on in laboratories.

I've often thought I'd quite like a white rat as a pet, just to get to know it and treat it kindly. My Jack Russell terrier would probably have other ideas though.

*

I found a dead rat in our woodshed,
I found it at quarter to eight,
I tried to give it the kiss of life,
But I'd left it ten minutes too late.

Waspishness

I wrote this at a time, decades ago, when I was under pressure to 'Get the next book out for Christmas' and I was beginning to realise that writing, which had always been so joyful to me, could under the wrong circumstances be turned into a deadline-driven chore. That was before I learned to resist bullying, before I had the lovely supportive, encouraging gang around me that I have now.

I am also embarrassed by the lack of knowledge shown here. Throughout the piece I refer to wasps as 'him' but of course worker wasps are all females. I also realise now, which I didn't before, that in many ways wasps are a tremendous force for good. They collect countless caterpillars to feed the larvae in their nests and these larvae, by way of a thank you, exude small, sugar-rich droplets of liquid, which feed the wasps. This exchange works a treat until the end of summer, when the number of larvae decreases and the wasps, no longer able to enjoy this sweet liquid, start to pester picnickers. For most of the year they do really good work, so I was wrong to write about them so unkindly. I should also compliment them on their nests, which are curvaceous and exquisitely made.

The blue bag mentioned at the end was a strange, universally employed aid used by our mothers on washing day. It was a round block of synthetic French Ultramarine tied tightly in muslin, the idea being that it imparted a blue tint, which by counteracting yellowing made the whites look brighter. Curiously, it was also the first thing reached for, wetted and slapped on in the event of a wasp or bee sting; the alkalinity was believed to ease the pain.

The Wasp He Is a Nasty One

The wasp he is a nasty one, he scavenges and thrives,
Unlike the honest honey bee, he doesn't care for hives,
He builds his waxy nest then brings his mates from near and far,
To sneak into your house when you have left the door ajar.

Then sniffing round for jam he goes in every pot and packet,
Buzzing round the kitchen in his black and yellow jacket,
If, with a rolled-up paper, he should spot you creeping near,
He'll do a backward somersault and sting you on the ear!

You never know with wasps, you can't relax, not for a minute,
Whatever you pick up – look out! A wasp might still be in it!
You never even know if there's a wasp against your chest,
For wasps are very fond of getting folded in your vest.

He always comes in summer, in the wintertime he's gone,
When you never go on picnics and you've put a jersey on,
What other single comment causes panic and despair,
Than someone saying, 'Keep still, there's a wasp caught in your
    hair!'

But in a speeding car he finds his favourite abode,
He likes poor Dad to swat like mad, and veer across the road,
He likes to watch Dad's face as all the kids begin to shout:
'Dad! I don't like wasps! Oh where's he gone Dad? Get him out!'

I'd like to make a reference to all the men who say,
'Don't antagonise it and the wasp will go away,'
I've done a little survey, to see if it will or won't,
And they sting you if you hit them, and they sting you if you
    don't.

As we step into the sunshine through the summers and the
    springs,
Carrying our cardigans and nursing all our stings,
I often wonder, reaching for the blue bag just once more,
If all things have a purpose … what on earth can wasps be for?

The Healesville Sanctuary

I first toured Australia in 1978 and I have enjoyed performing there and getting to know that sensational country regularly ever since. My most recent visit was in 2020, although then my shows in Adelaide and Perth were cancelled due to the Covid pandemic and a lovely, relaxed amble round Australia turned into a desperate scramble to get home.

I've always felt strongly that it is a great privilege to work in a different country alongside real people who live there. I've never much enjoyed being a tourist in a new country, being chaperoned round the sights by someone with a flag and an itinerary, and being herded on and off the bus.

When you're working in a country to perform a series of theatre dates, it is usual for those dates to be packed closely together to keep down the cost of accommodation for everyone involved in putting on the show. Frustratingly, this often means rushing past interesting places where you would have loved to linger. Days off are few and precious.

During my first Australian tour I was due to play a theatre in Melbourne, and we had one free day. A visit had been arranged to the Healesville Sanctuary, a type of zoo. At that time I found it a depressing place, the animals just there to be gawped at in mean cages and enclosures, seemingly with no thought of what they needed to stay sane. There was a sad porcupine-like echidna, which ran endlessly and desperately round and round the four bare walls of its run, never ceasing. The soulless confinement had driven it nuts.

Now, over forty years later, the Healesville Sanctuary is a very different place indeed. It fights to prevent wildlife extinction and has successful breeding programmes for the duck-billed platypus and other members of Australia's uniquely special and magical fauna. Rich natural habitats are provided for its residents, and for the casualties it takes in and treats. Today it bears no relation to the place I first saw.

On that day in the Healesville Sanctuary in 1978, I first set eyes on a duck-billed platypus. Like much else it was housed in miserable accommodation, a kind of glass coffin mounted on a stand in which the shy, luckless platypus undulated back and forth looking for a place to hide. This lack of any shelter meant you could get a good look at it, and it seemed to me to be the most bizarre collection of ingredients ever assembled. It was furry, with a vast comical beak, webbed feet, venomous spikes, and the ability to lay eggs from which bean-sized babies hatch and are nursed by the mother.

The thought occurred to me that perhaps God had made the duck-billed platypus from all the pieces he had left over when he'd finished making everybody else …

How God Made the Duck-Billed Platypus

The duck-billed platypus, small aquatic friend,
Made from the pieces God had over at the end,
According to His reckoning (He'd not been wrong before),
He hadn't made enough: He needed one mammal more.

He studied all the corners of his cupboard, large and bare,
A little foot here, and a little nose there,
A scrap of fur, a feather, nothing anyone would miss,
And God said, 'Oh good God … Yes? … What can I make
　　out of this?'

There was a funny flat tail and a great enormous beak,
Which had lain in the cupboard for a year and a week,
There were four webbed feet in the manner of a duck,
And hanging on a peg, a furry overcoat for luck!

So the turn of the platypus came to be fitted,
God sat him down and he honestly admitted,
That the finished platypus might appear a little odd,
'But look on the bright side of it,' said God.

'You can swim in the river, you can paddle in the creek,
You can tackle anybody with a great big beak!
There's a tail for a rudder or alternatively legs,
And by way of consolation you've got babies *and* eggs.'

So God took all the pieces into Workshop One,
And there he told the men the sort of thing he wanted done,
The Carpenter and Plumber stroked the platypus's neck,
And said, 'Don't you upset him, he can't run but he can peck!'

So the platypus was made, and his beak was firmly rooted,
And God found him a home where he would not be persecuted,
They packed him up and sent him, with his tail neatly furled,
In a brown paper parcel marked 'Australia, The World'.

I'm the Dog Who Didn't Win a Prize

I hate judging things because afterwards the winner regards you with adoration, while all the other contestants give you a nasty look. These days I avoid judging anything but years ago, before I decided on this policy, I was invited to a fundraising day at a dogs' home in Evesham, Worcestershire. There were various stalls and tea and cakes, but the highlight of the day was a light-hearted dog show featuring classes like Dog with the Waggiest Tail, Dog the Judge Would Most Like to Take Home, Best Taker of the Tit-Bit, that sort of thing. My job was to walk round with their good-looking vet and help with the judging. When it came to the Most Beautiful Bitch class, I gave the prize to a little dog with a sweet face and exceptionally dark, appealing eyes. Afterwards the vet told me that it had some eye disorder, one symptom of which is that the eyes appear particularly large and moist. This made me wonder if I was the right woman for the job, but overall it was a pleasant, sunny day, which raised money for a good cause.

As the event wound up, families began to drift away, with many of the dogs sporting rosettes and ribbons to show off when they arrived home. One small, disgruntled-looking dog passed, and he seemed to look back over his shoulder at me in an indignant and miffed fashion. He was a little, dark, long-haired dog of the dachshund type, with large, tufted ears. And no rosette.

I'm the dog who didn't win a prize,
I didn't have the 'Most Appealing Eyes',
All day in this heat, I've been standing on me feet,
With dogs of every other shape and size.

I've been harshly disinfected, I've been scrubbed,
I've been festooned in a towel and I've been rubbed,
I've been mercilessly brushed, robbed of all me fleas and dust,
And now the judging's over: I've been snubbed!

Was it for obedience I was hailed?
As 'Best Dog in the Show' was I regaled?
O not on your Doggo life, such unfairness, it is rife!
I had one thing said about me – it was 'FAILED'.

I never for a moment thought I'd fail,
I thought at least I'd win 'Waggiest Tail',
But no certificate, rosette or commendation did I get –
Nothing on a kennel door to nail.

I am going in my kennel on my own.
Thank you, no. I do not want a bone.
Do not think you can console me, with leftovers in my bowl,
My pride is mortified – I want to be alone.

I've heard it from the worldly and the wise:
'Each dog has his day' they all advise,
But I see to my grief and sorrow, my day must have been
    tomorrow!
For I'm the dog who didn't win a prize.

Tiger, Tiger

The tiger that stalks through the night
Delivers a hideous bite
And there on his paws
Are razor-sharp claws
Apart from all that, he's all right!

The Ballad of the Bungleclud

I do like the Bungleclud and am glad to find that children are fond of him as well. It must be something to do with him liking to have the English teacher for tea …

*

In the marshes, thick with mud,
Lies the dreadful Bungleclud,
In the bog up to his eyes,
There he watches, there he spies,
Still, except for fingers drumming,
Looking out for people coming.

Bunglecluds are large and hairy,
And their eyes are quick and wary,
Watching out for signs of joggers,
Ice-cream men, or stray hot-doggers,
English teachers, you or me,
Or anyone to have for tea.

Bunglecluds are dark and wrinkled,
And their tails are long and crinkled,
On their ears are tufts of hair,
That twitch and flicker everywhere,
And both their nostrils, red and flared,
Are good for making people scared.

But oh, his mouth so wide and black,
With great big tonsils down the back,
And jagged teeth from left to right,
No fillings, caps or crowns in sight,
And Bunglebreath, so foul and smelly,
Turns most people's knees to jelly.

Lying in the mud so long,
Causes Bunglecluds to pong,
When it gets too much to bear,
Up they get and out they tear,
Climbing madly up the trees,
To have an airing in the breeze.

When Bunglecluds no longer hum,
Down to earth refreshed they come,
They promenade along the grass,
And to Bunglecluds they pass,
Enquire 'How is your sainted mother?'
And sweetly smile at one another.

Bunglecluds are rarely seen,
But anywhere that mud is green,
And deep and dark and nasty smelling,
Go with caution! There's no telling!
Bubbles rise from the deep …
Could mean a Bungleclud … Asleep!

Fleeced

We kept a few sheep for a long time but, looking back, I don't think I was ever that good at being a shepherd. My sheep weren't neglected but, certainly at first, I had no idea how much work was involved in looking after them properly. For instance, in the winter their cloven hooves react badly to mud, and they get malodorous foot infections. You have to tip them over onto their backs, cut away the nasty parts and treat the foot with antibiotic spray. Obviously, the sheep doesn't take to this indignity and the struggle while bent double is taxing, especially if, like us, you have chosen to keep a great big sheep like the Cotswold, in which case you need the strength of Hercules. They weren't known as Cotswold Lions for nothing. Then they need shearing, treating against flystrike, which is the polite name for maggots, help with lambing when necessary and innumerable other services. Sheep aren't something to take on lightly. You need a kind but tough approach. Ours were never destined for the freezer. They just stood around looking nice, grew old, incurred large vets bills and then died, causing me to collapse in floods of tears. So, on balance, no, I don't think I was really cut out for the job.

I bought a flock of sheep because my garden seemed so bare,
I thought they'd eat the grass and add a touch of interest there,
The soil was alkali, and there were mice and there were ants,
So I thought I'd get some sheep because the frost had my
 chrysanths.

First, they ate the grass and then the borders and the shrubs,
The blue and white lobelia, the alpines in the tubs,
I had to get some grazing to accommodate my sheep,
With shelter and a water trough, and none of it came cheap.

I love my little flock, but I have had to come to terms,
With dipping, shearing, dagging, dosing, drenching them for
 worms,
And on a winter's afternoon not dozing by the fire,
But trying to free a sheep that's got its head stuck in the wire.

And then they get diseases, they get fluke and they get mange,
They get foot rot, they get orf, they might get scrapie for a
    change,
And when it comes to lambing time, the nights are cold and
    black,
With you, the soapy water, and a lamb with both legs back.

Consider very carefully before you buy a sheep,
They need much supervision, and you won't get any sleep,
You'll have to pay the rent, the vet, the drugs, the food, the licks,
And learn to be adept at extricating bloated ticks.

If you keep a ram, yes, he'll look noble in the clover,
Though when your back is turned, he'll do his best to knock you
    over,
But if without a flock of sheep, you'll waste away and pine,
Then come and talk to me as I should like to give you mine.

The Horse's Farewell to His Cowboy

People often ask me which is my favourite poem out of all the ones I've written, and for a long time I would have said this one. It is so daft, and was so great to perform, to play the poor stricken horse and feel the righteous rage of the audience towards that low, unfeeling rotter of a cowboy who never took care of his long-suffering old steed or gave him the love he deserved. I've always felt that 'And as from tonight, he can bloody well walk' was a great come-uppance line at the end. Yeah, that cold-hearted cowboy – serves him right!

Farewell to you cowboy, my day it is done,
Of rounding up cows in the heat of the sun,
Of roping the dogies and branding the steer,
And having your gun going off in my ear.

I galloped the prairie without any thanks,
Your great silver spurs in my bony old flanks,
And I've seen many things in my life it is true,
But never a cowboy more stupid than you.

Chorus:
Cowboy can you hear me inside the saloon?
I'm waiting out here in the light of the moon,
My hardworking days they are past and gone by,
And I'm bound for the great clover field in the sky.

Farewell to the feel of your filthy old jeans,
Farewell to the smell of your coffee and beans,
Farewell to you in your Stetson and chaps,
Cheating at poker and shooting the craps.

You rode me too fast and you rode me too far,
Mile after mile of you shouting 'Yee har!'
Hounded by outlaws away down the track,
With a gun on my tail and a berk on my back.

I never remember you treating me right,
I was tied to a cactus and hungry all night,
When I was weary and dying of thirst,
I always knew it was you who came first.

Well maybe you are mighty quick on the draw,
But cowboy you're slow with the fodder and straw,
Look at me pardner, I'm all skin and bone,
So tonight I ride into the sunset … alone.

He'll have a shock when he comes out of there,
Me, with four legs sticking up in the air,
Don't say goodbye, or thanks for the ride,
My friend it's too little, too late. I have died.

Won't somebody lift up the old saddle flaps,
And gently unbuckle the filthy old straps,
My eyes have grown weary, I'm tired of talk,
And as from tonight, he can bloody well walk.

FREEDOM FROM FEAR

The Insects' Anthem

This is a song to be performed to the tune of 'The Ballad of Jimmy Brown' also known as 'Three Bells'.

I love this. Reading through it, some decades after I wrote it, I think it was ahead of its time. I am glad that people are kinder to insects now and see their importance in the scheme of things. I always imagine this being sung by a vast cast of insects lined up across a stage, antennae and wing-cases quivering with indignation at the unjust, murderous treatment meted out to them down the centuries.

ROLL OF HONOUR

EARWIGS   10,000
CENTIPEDES 20,000
THICK-THIGHED
FLOWER BEETLE 10,000
YELLOW MEADOW... COUNTLESS
ANTS

We. We the assembled,
Do hereby pledge a solemn vow,
If any of us be faint-hearted,
Let him leave the party now.
Our comrades all have gone to glory,
We will not see their like again,
They figured briefly in life's story,
And now are numbered, with the slain.

We are gathered here together,
Recalling creatures great and small,
Their names are on the roll of honour,
Here upon the garden wall,
These are the heroes of our nation,
These are the victims of the spray,
Those who fell in rotovation,
And all forms of cultivation,
We remember them today.

 Friends. Friends and neighbours,
All those dependent on the soil,
We, whose lives are overshadowed,
In every aspect of our toil,
For those who cling to vegetation,
Inhabitants of bean and pea,
Those, who wade upon the water,
And those in peril … up a tree.

We see them bearing down upon us,
Armed with their implements and hoes,
We see them marching down the furrows,
To give us all a bloody nose,
We live in fear of persecution,
Our song of freedom must be sung,
Those of us they have beheaded,
Pruned and composted and shredded,
Lie abandoned in the dung.

So, in condemnation,
Of evil deeds and slaughter foul,
Those, so murderously taken,
By the dibble and the trowel,
For those who tremble in the darkness,
For those in grassy roots below,
Who dread the whistle of the strimmer,
And the man who went to mow.

Weevils, mites and hairy spiders,
Aphids, ladybirds and bees,
Gather round in supplication,
On their bended hairy knees,
From the bondage of oppression,
We will one day all be free,
Every creepy every crawly,
Every martyr gone to glory,
In the name of liberty …
(heroic big finish)
Liberty, Libertee, Li-ber-TEEEEEEEE!*

*A flag may be waved at
  this dramatic moment.

To Make a Whale

Man is gloriously clever,
Making intricate machines,
And complicated gadgetry,
And bigger runner beans,
And journeys into space,
With mighty rockets in the tail …
But when the last one's towed away,
He couldn't make a whale.

When I Get Up from My Chair

Here is a gardener with plans, feverish plans. He is going to be unstoppable, a mighty force! He will take on all those pesky insects, his garden is going to look wondrous, there's going to be a transformation!

Well, there will be, in a minute or two ... once he gets up from his chair.

Quiet please! Kindly don't impede my concentration,
I am sitting in the garden thinking thoughts of propagation,
Of sowing and of nurturing, the fruits my work will bear,
And the place won't know what hit it ... Once I get up from
my chair.

I'm at the planning stages now, if you should need to ask,
And if I'm looking weary, it's the rigours of the task,
The making of a garden is a strain, as you can guess,
So if my eyes should close, it isn't sleep of course ... It's stress.

Oh the leeks that I will dibble and the beans that I will stick,
The bugs that I will slaughter and the seedlings I will prick,
I'll disinfect the greenhouse, I will organise the shed,
And beside my faded roses I will snip off every head.

The mower I will cherish and the tools that I will oil,
The dark nutritious compost I will stroke into the soil,
My sacrifice, devotion and heroic aftercare,
Will leave you green with envy ... Once I get up from my chair.

Oh the weeds that I shall mutilate, the clumps that I will split,
I'm foaming at the mouth just at the very thought of it,
I am heaving at the traces, I am tearing out my hair,
And you'll see a ruddy hero ... Once I get up from my chair.

I will massacre the bindweed and the moss upon the lawn,
That hairy bittercress will curse the day that it was born,
I will rise against the foe and in the fight, we will be matched,
And the woolly caterpillars, they will curse the day they hatched.

Oh the branches I will layer and the cuttings I will take,
Let other fellows dig a pond – *I* shall dig a lake!
My garden, what a showpiece! There'll be pilgrims come to stare,
And I'll bow, and take the credit ...
    Once I get up from my chair.

Keeping Chickens

I like to keep a few laying hens, and I certainly did when our children were small. I kept them for two reasons: firstly, because I would know that the eggs produced were from birds humanely kept and wholesomely fed and, secondly, when one of the hens went broody, I intended to give her a clutch of fertile eggs to sit on. This would enable our children to see the chicks hatch, a charming and educational experience, and the whole family could enjoy watching the mother hen cluck round the garden with her family. This is what I hoped.

I wanted to recreate some of the excitement I had felt myself, long ago in Stanford in the Vale, when my mother used to send away for day-old chicks. They came by train in a stout square box perforated with round holes. Mum would call us in, the box would be on the kitchen table, and she would say, 'Hark! What can you hear?' Through the silence would come a magical cheep-cheep from inside the box and there was great joy as the little chicks were taken out, stroked, sniffed and inspected. My sister and I used to take a hammer and bash up wheat for them on the front doorstep, which created a nutritious mixture of crushed wheat and stone dust. You can see that this is a nice memory for me, I like it, I'm glad to have it, and I wanted to create a little bit of something similar for my own family.

It was not so easy. In the 1950s it was simple to buy the chickens you wanted. I remember running my fingers down the poultry section of the classified adverts and seeing plenty of entries for our sort of birds. It would say RIR X LS and to the chicken-literate this meant a cross between a brown bird called the Rhode Island Red and a whitish one called the Light Sussex. This combination gave you a personable girl who, given plenty of encouragement and mother's mash, would lay well.

But now I couldn't find any. Not a single RIR X LS was advertised anywhere. In the intervening years chicken breeding had become much more scientific. Commercial egg producers, with some justification, do not want birds that go broody. Going broody means that they stop laying and sit tight on any eggs they can find. To the businessman this represents loss of production and so the bird most frequently offered nowadays is a thing called the Black Rock. In my opinion the Black Rock is a non-chicken. It is not the rich conker brown of the Rhode Island Red, who has great feathery knickers down her legs and a knowing eye. It is a vile plum colour, like claret and mud. It is a machine. It has no maternal instinct. It has a computer-programmed sort of look in its eye. It turns up, fires out the eggs, exhausts itself and keels over, whereupon the businessman ships in some more. I looked at the Black Rock and thought, 'No way, mush,' and resolved to look further afield.

My search took me to a superior sort of establishment, which bred and offered for sale old traditional breeds of farm animals: pigs, sheep and particularly poultry. They had all manner of ducks and fancy turkeys. They had geese and guinea fowl. They had Rhode Island Reds and I bought six. The cost was prohibitive. I had to put my name on a long waiting list. It was like ordering one of those posey dogs that real dogs laugh at.

At last, the chickens arrived. I had bought a house and all the equipment. I had natty galvanised hoppers for the food, hygienic drinkers, quantities of the proper grit they need for rock-hard eggshells and the finest additive-free feed from a joint twelve miles away in Tetbury. These chickens were feather-bedded.

I put them into their quarters and wafted away, happy. Wafting back, I found one had a bad leg. She was standing in the corner of the run with an imploring look on her face, holding the gammy leg up in her feathers. I examined it and, clearly, she was unable to put one foot to the ground at all. As they had cost so much I thought it worth taking her to the vet. I put her under my arm and knocked on the door of his surgery. He manipulated the bird's joint and agreed that it was inflamed. He administered an anti-inflammatory injection to her and a substantial bill to me. I took the chicken home, but she did not get better. This took a little of the gloss off the poultry operation.

More gloss came off shortly afterwards when another bird fell sick. On top of her head a chicken should have a nice glossy red comb, which sticks up proudly and shines with rude health. Should the comb flop over and turn grey, trouble is afoot. A second stricken chicken emerged. Not only did she have a grey, flabby-looking comb like a slab of old bacon, but her breathing was noisy and tormented. I picked her up and we stared at each other, eye to eye. Each rattling and agonised breath seemed likely to be her last. In my hands she was hot and limp. I took her to the vet as well.

'Where did you get these chickens?' he demanded as if they were something nasty from under the counter.

I told him.

'I'm beginning to think you might have something viral in your flock,' he said. 'You're not thinking of breeding from these birds, are you?'

'No,' I lied.

'Because I couldn't recommend it at all.'

'Great,' I thought.

'However,' he said, 'we will do what we can. This bird is suffering from inflammation of the respiratory tract. I will give you some yellow powder to put in the water and you must treat them all to prevent the spread of infection. Is that clear?'

It was becoming clear to me that it was a sight easier to buy your eggs from Tesco like everybody else.

I took the yellow powder and the substantial bill, came home and treated the water. I watched my flock for improvement, but I watched in vain.

Not long after that, and I know some people will think I am making this up but I'm not, a third bird became sick. This one was gross, the worst of all. In front of her eye she developed a hard, hot, pulsating swelling. This caused the actual eyeball to foam and froth. It was truly horrible to look at. She squinted at me with a troubled air. I just could not keep a bird in that condition. The vet seemed strangely pleased to see me. 'Come in!' he gushed.

He said that, indeed, the whole flock had a viral infection and that, if I wanted to, I could probably take up the legal cudgels with the supplier. In the meantime, he would do what he could. He gave me a phial of eye drops and a set of three pre-filled hypodermic syringes to be administered on three consecutive days. And a bill.

I don't know if you have ever tried to put eye drops in a chicken's eye, but you need a steady hand and a willing chicken, and I had neither. On first detecting the cold liquid in her eye she shook her head so violently that, although unafflicted myself, I got the full benefit of the treatment. Then I had to turn her over and inject her with the syringe. I had never injected anything in my life. It was like Sunday dinner with the feathers on. A fiasco.

I used to have this vision. In it, I wear a print dress and walk in the sunshine. Over my arm there is a basket with sweet hay nestling in the base. I step along the garden path until I reach a coop of contented chickens, clucking and fluffing up their feathers in a dust-bath. Lifting the sun-warmed lid of the nest boxes I see, to my delight, speckled eggs, warm and fulsome. These I place reverently into my basket. Smiling, I turn and walk away with skirt billowing, until my figure is obscured and swallowed up in the hollyhocks.

The reality is harsher. The sky is grey and lowering. I am plodding across a wet field with a bucket. I am wearing my husband's Drizabone coat and the dog has chewed the hem, causing it to hang in rags. I reach the beleaguered chicken coop, there are no eggs, and I didn't fancy them anyway. I fling open the door and there they are, my six chickens. One has a leg up in its feathers, it can't walk it can only hop. Another is breathing great ragged breaths, beak agape. The third is staring up at me from behind a great carbuncle. As they glare at me accusingly, I hear the vet drive past in his Mercedes.

With These Hands

I came late to motherhood and it was a shock. Prior to our first son being born I had led a fairly self-indulgent life with plenty of sleep and plenty of options. I had lots of time to perfect the hairdo, anoint myself with fragrant lotions, go out and about and do exactly as I pleased.

All this was blown apart when, at the age of thirty-five I gave birth to a little son. It was replaced by the torture of continuous sleepless nights, the desperate bafflement I felt when confronted by this little person who cried and cried but could not tell me what was wrong, and shattered, bone-weary exhaustion.

Above and beyond that, though, came the astounding new kind of love which places everything else in perspective, the realisation that *this* is what matters, this family and its survival. Perhaps, for the first time, I could see the shallowness of what had gone before. It also dawned on me that now I would be called upon to acquire new skills and plenty of them, particularly with regard to an assortment of miscellaneous pets …

With these hands so soft and clean,
On which I stroke the Vaseline,
I soothe the fever, cool the heat,
Lift verrucas out of feet,
Slap the plasters on the knees,
Dig the garden, prune the trees,
And if it doesn't work at all,
I throw the mower at the wall.

With these hands I crack the eggs,
Floss my teeth, shave my legs,
Write the cheques, count the fivers,
Make rude signs at piggish drivers,
Clean the goldfish, light the fires,
Pump up half a dozen tyres,
Feed the hamster, worm the dog,
And decorate the Yuletide log.

With these hands I block the lens,
When taking photos of my friends,
This is Mary, this is Fred,
See their eyeballs all gone red,
With them I gesticulate,
I wag a finger, say, 'You're late!'
Throw them up, say, 'Don't ask me!'
And, 'What's that in your hand? Let's see!'

With these hands I fondly make,
A brontosaurus birthday cake,
I'm sorry for the shape it's in,
But half of it stuck in the tin.
I pop the corn, I pick the mix,
I whack the cricket ball for six,
I organise the party game,
And clean up things too vile to name.

No pair of jeans do I refuse,
No Levis, Wranglers or FUs,
I wash them fast, I mend them quick,
I sew through denim hard and thick,
For no repair job makes me frown,
I take them up, I let them down,
I do the fly, I do the rip,
I do the knee, I do the zip.

And with these hands I dab the eyes,
Officiate at fond goodbyes,
As in the earth we gravely dig,
The late lamented guinea pig,
I bow my head, cross my chest,
And lay his furry soul to rest,
Reflecting that, on many a day,
I could have helped him on his way.

I greet the folk who bang the door,
Fill the mouths that shout for more,
Scrape the trainers free of muck,
Gut the fish and stuff the duck,
I cart the shopping, heave the coal,
Stick the plunger down the bowl,
Take foreign bodies from the eye,
And with these hands I wave
                                        Goodbye.

The Pike in the Pub

When I worked as a secretary for Smiths Industries in Witney in the 1970s, I used to go for a walk at lunchtime. If I got a move on, I could walk down the road towards Crawley, turn left through a strip of woodland with the rather macabre name of Maggots Grove and reach the sparkling River Windrush, now heavily and foully polluted.

One summer's day, in a shallow drainage channel leading into the main stream, I saw the backs of two large pike sticking out of the water, side by side, sunning themselves in a companiable way. Sensing my approach, they were gone in a quick frantic splash, but it was so nice to see. Apparently sunbathing is a popular pike pastime.

I am not a fan of fish in glass cases, varnished, embellished with fake reeds and annotated with date of death. I would rather they were still alive, motionless under the tree roots somewhere, in a deep dark pool along the river.

LAKE BALA
MCH 11th, 1931

A pike patrolled this waterway, intent upon predation,
His appetite unparalleled in this or any nation,
Until a roving fisherman with courage, skill and class,
Installed him, fellow drinkers, safe within these walls of glass.

Walking to Falkirk

During the nineteenth century, Highland cattle, having reached maturity on the island of Skye, would be taken to the cattle markets of Falkirk on the mainland. The only way for them to get there was to walk, and when they reached the intervening stretch of water they were made to swim. A rope passing beneath the tongue was secured around the lower jaw and the animals were towed behind rowing boats to reach the opposite shore.

I like Highland cattle with their thick fringes, wide horns and big pink noses, and I think they would have found this treatment a serious affront to their dignity …

*

I am just not looking forward to this journey to Falkirk,
I have tried to get excited but I can't, it doesn't work,
Three hundred miles of walking south, *walking* night and day!
Plodding over Scotland, udders swinging all the way.

Well I'm not going, I'm not going, as a rule I'm kind and nice,
But I'm not built for endurance, I won't go at any price.

Well, what a thing to ask of me, of me and all my friends!
Imagine our discomfort as we hobble through the glens,
The flies! The deprivations! And as if that weren't enough,
We'd have to eat the heather, and it's stringy! And it's tough!

So I'm not going, I'm not going, I won't plunge or go berserk,
But I'm no long-distance runner, I'm not walking to Falkirk.

It's come to my attention that upon the drovers' whim,
They tip us in the briny and encourage us to *swim*!
I'd have no shred of dignity! I'm much too highly strung,
To be towed behind a rowboat with a rope beneath my tongue!

No, I'm not going, I'm not walking, I'm not flailing through the
    mud,
I'll be found beneath my shady tree, chewing on the cud.

In fact I've ruminated here from underneath my fringe,
And have devised a policy to make the drover cringe,
So when he comes to get me on a frosty Highland morn,
I'll be waiting with a welcome! With a welcome from my horns!

Yes, see the drover fly! There go his sporran and his dirk,
'Cause I'm not walking, I'm not walking, I'm NOT WALKING to
    Falkirk.

Adopting a Dog

Our dog died. We'd had her for twelve years. She came from a dogs' home startlingly named The Sombrero, in Droitwich, where she was optimistically described as a 'Labrador type'. She was entirely sweet-natured, and when our two small sons were growing up, there was always a threesome to be seen around the place, comprised of two little boys and a dog, with a ball or stick for the entertainment of all parties. Years later she became ill and frail and one morning we came downstairs and found she had died.

I always keep a towel for each of my dogs to dry them when they come in wet, so we wrapped her up in her own blue towel, my sons dug a grave for her in the garden and we buried her and everyone cried. What touched me so much was the tenderness with which my great eighteen-year-old son arranged the towel across her face so that the soil wouldn't go into her eyes. By a dismal piece of timing, that night I had five hundred people in a theatre in Essex waiting for a good laugh.

After a time, we got used to the idea that she had gone, but we all missed our big dog, and our Jack Russell terrier Tatty was lonely and had nobody to stand underneath. She's called Tatty because every hair that grows in her coat comes out at a different angle; my husband says she looks like a lavatory brush. So, we had space for another large dog and, knowing that the dogs' homes are full of brilliant pets waiting for another chance, I drove up to the Blue Cross in nearby Burford to see what dogs were available.

If you viewed the place from above it would look like a cake, with the actual kennels in the centre and the runs radiating out like wedges, so you can walk all the way round and see the dogs inside. Some runs have two dogs, others only one, and there are balls and rubber bones lying around but they don't seem to get played with much.

Some dogs looked savage and snarled, others seemed cowed and frightened. I came to a great smiling golden retriever called Hattie who waved her fine tail, but when I asked about her I found she'd just been adopted by another family. I went back out and walked round until I came to a different dog and stopped. It barked nervously at me. It was a very odd-looking dog. Immensely tall and spindly, with long black ears, a black saddle and strange dappled spots, she was painfully thin with the bumps of her spine sticking up all along her back. Round the run was a blue-and-white cordon like the ones the police put round a crime scene, and on it someone had written in black felt-tip pen: 'Do not approach this dog. This dog may have ringworm.' Other people passing exclaimed with distaste, 'Urgh, *ringworm!*'

The dog stood in a shallow puddle of disinfectant in the newly cleansed run, and looked the most lonely, heartbroken, baffled animal I had ever seen. I thought: 'That dog looks daft enough to be our dog!'

I went back into the office and enquired about her, saying: 'I like the look of that black-and-white mongrel, the one that might have ringworm.'

The man said, 'Oh no, dear, oh no. That dog is no mongrel. *She* is a LARGE MUNSTERLANDER.'

I looked at him blankly. I had never heard of it. Apparently, it is a German gun-dog breed, developed in and around the area of Munster.

I said, 'What's her name?'

The man said, 'Ella.'

I thought about it. 'I don't like that name much, for a dog,' I said, 'it's sort of wishy-washy. If I had her, do you think I could call her something else?'

'Oh yes, dear,' he said, 'you can call her anything you like but she won't know who you're talking to.'

That made perfectly good sense. I told him we would like to offer her a home.

Now, if you adopt a dog from a dogs' home, you are not allowed to just clip on a lead and walk out with it. Many of the dogs have had a poor start, so the staff need to feel fairly sure that you will be a better bet, that you and the dog will suit each other. To this end you are asked to comply with several procedures. First, they like to see any other dogs which live in your home and introduce them to the new dog on neutral ground, to see if they are going to get along. Somewhat nervously I went home and fetched Tatty. She marched in, chest out, saying, 'The bigger they come, the harder they fall …' but on seeing the stupendous size of the other dog, she decided to be friendly. They ran after a ball together and didn't fall out.

Next, you are asked to bring in all the members of the family who live at home. You stand in a line and they look in your ears to see if you've got canker. No, I made that up, they don't do that really; they just like to meet everyone, I suppose to see if there are any dissenters. After that, an inspector comes out to your house to see if your garden is secure, that the dog can't get out onto a busy road for instance, and they check for other possible hazards. Eventually all this was done, and we were told that we could have Ella. We had to wait for her to be spayed as it's the policy of the home to neuter all dogs, and one day we went in our car to collect her and bring her home, duly embroidered.

When we got her home, I began to realise just what we had taken on. She was ten months old and had received no training at all. She took no notice of anything you said to her, she wasn't housetrained, and she stole food. If you were unwise enough to leave a delicious roast leg of lamb on the worktop she would stroll up and, enabled by her enormous height, help herself and say, 'Well, this is dashed good of the old gal.'

One day I made a Victoria sandwich. I had a lot of people coming to tea, so I doubled the recipe to make a big one. On the beautiful fluted, golden-brown base, I spread thickly whipped double cream. Over that I smoothed a generous layer of my own blackcurrant jam. One ran down the other in a voluptuous dribble. Then I positioned the lovely golden top, placed the cake on a pretty china stand and dredged the whole glorious edifice with a snowy dusting of icing sugar. It was a work of art. It looked like a picture in a magazine. I left it on the worktop and went upstairs to get the washing.

When I came down, it was to a scene of utter desecration. I honestly thought I was seeing things. The whole cake had been smashed down onto the floor and reduced to a swirled creamy mess of chunks, crumbs and jammy paw prints. The big dog, her long black nose covered in cream back to the eyes, was saying, 'It was nothing to do with me, I don't eat cake.' Tatty, moustache bristling with crumbs, was saying, 'Quick! Get some more down here!'

I decided I needed some help. I rang the vet, explained the situation and asked if he knew of a good dog trainer.

'This lady seems to be well thought of,' he said. 'I'll give you the number.'

I rang the lady and told her about Ella. She paused, fetched her diary and said, yes, she could come out on Thursday and train me. Me, you notice.

On Thursday she duly arrived, and I was taken aback. She came in a big truck and was herself a large, forthright woman.

'Morning!' she boomed. 'Morning, Mrs Russell!'

Russell is my married name. My husband has been called Mr Ayres for twenty-three years and it gets on his wick.

She inspected the dog and announced: 'Now, the first thing I observe about your dog, Mrs Russell, is that your dog does not come back when you call it!'

I had observed that for myself.

'As such,' she went on, 'your dog is a menace to itself and to everybody else! So today we will work on the Recall. THE RECALL! I want you to attach your dog to a long rope and then I want you to SPRINT across the field in the direction of the OAK TREE, while BLOWING your WHISTLE, and calling your dog's name ENTHUSIASTICALLY! When you reach the tree, I want you to BOB DOWN and PROFFER THE TITBIT! OFF YOU GO!'

Well, I didn't know if I was on foot or horseback. The dog was so immensely strong she nearly pulled my arm OFF. I was trying to blow the whistle and gasp out the dog's name at the same time, while behind me the lady shrilled, 'She can't HEAR you!' It was a nightmare. I felt so uncoordinated and humiliated. This went on for three weeks, after which it was decided that I would now continue on my own and try to put into practice what I had been shown. That was the situation when a terrible thing happened.

My husband had taken the dog out last thing at night for a wee. I thought they had been gone a long time and I began to have misgivings. After far too long a wait, the back door was kicked open. In came my husband, all red in the face. He was blazing. His eyes stood out as he shouted: 'The bloody dog's run off!'

Then, well you can guess what came next, he bawled: 'I never wanted the BLOODY DOG in THE FIRST PLACE!'

'Oh no? Well, you might have mentioned that before NOW!'

Anyway, the dog had gone. She's a gun dog who had spent the first ten months of her life in London, starved of any of the exciting smells she was bred to follow. All round us there are multitudes of rabbits and foxes. She had sniffed the heady, irresistible, late-night scents, shaken off her collar and vanished.

The whole family rushed outside. It was late and foggy. Everywhere there was a still silence. There was no yelp, no excited bark, no helpful snapping of twigs under galloping paws. Only the fog and deadly quiet. It was terrible.

We came in. I phoned the police and the dog warden in Swindon. We live surrounded by livestock. A loose dog is the worst thing. For all I knew, ours could have been dragging the throats out of all the neighbouring sheep. Or our own sheep. It was terrifying. The whole family at that late hour went out to look for her. My husband went off in his car and our two sons went off in their various vehicles. I could see the headlights in the fog, criss-crossing the surrounding fields, driving slowly along the edges of the woods. We searched all night. I was the last to give up at a quarter to five in the morning. Prior to that I had been walking along the local roads with a big torch, shouting: 'ACHTUNG! Where are you, you great BRATWURST, come home!'

We never found her ourselves. The postman spotted her in a neighbouring field at about eleven o'clock the next morning. Filthy and exhausted, she must have run for miles and miles.

That was the low point. Since then, things have steadily improved and now you wouldn't recognise her. She has turned into one of those admirable, eager-to-please dogs which do as they are told, and the touching thing is she *loves* my husband. She absolutely adores him. She didn't hear what he said about her that night.

When he comes in from work at night, he is tired. He doesn't want to dance the salsa, he's weary. He likes to have his supper and sit down with the paper. He's got a green leather reclining armchair and he likes to sit with his feet up, cup of coffee on one side, paper on the other, TV in front, and he's perfectly happy. The dog watches him carefully until he is settled. Then, sinuous and snake-like, she pussyfoots over to him and lies down in a great curving arc close beside him. She rolls over on to her back with her four great hairy paws in the air and gazes up at him with an expression of devotion.

Unfortunately, she is a martyr to flatulence, and this can rather spoil the effect. Sometimes my husband doesn't have to turn the pages of the newspaper himself at all. Nevertheless, despite all this, I still have two dogs and one husband under the same roof. I hope my account has not discouraged you from adopting your own dog from a dogs' home. Ours has been well worth the effort.

Bonemeal

Bury me beside my dogs,
The dogs I loved and knew,
So, as in life, they'll never be,
Short of a bone to chew.

The Pig Epistle
(A psalm-like chant)

I would really like you to hear this sung, because the fun of it is
in trying to pack a great many words into a very short line.

*

And lo I saw before me the birds of the air and the beasts of
    all the field,
One among them stood forth, raised up his noble head and
    squealed,
He hath a great round nose, his skin all clad in bristle,
And so to the everlasting glory of the pig I give you this …
    epistle.

The pig hath a wondrous song, hearken to the grunting and
    the snort,
And in past times the catching of the greasy pig provided the
    youth of the village with much lively … sport,
Although the length of time they could hang on to it was not
    likely to be long,
And the fragrance left on those that tried was overwhelming …
    strong.

She walks with a delicate step and mighty swinging of the
    udder,
Those of a delicate sensibility may turn up their nose and
    shudder,

But while other species never produce offspring that number as
much as four,
The fertile and fecund sow regularly whips out a dozen or
more.

If someone offers you a sheep, you must decline with thanks
For verily the sheep she is as thick as two short planks,
Horses I have never liked, my uncle was to blame,
One kicked him in the teeth and then his smile was never the
same.

In the name of the sow, the boar, the piglet, hog and swine,
Placed evermore upon this Earth to flourish and to shine,
Hosanna to the pig, so noble and glorious in ever fibre,
His brethren shall populate the Earth from here to up the
Khyber.

As a lifelong friend and confidante, it sure is hard to beat it,
And yet when hardship strikes it's tough, but you can take a
knife and fork and … eat it,
When everyone is out to get you and your troubles seem awful
big,
Remember that stoutly in the backyard stands a loyal friend,
Always ready to lend a sympathetic ear,
His face all covered in mealy swill,
Remember the piiiiiiig.

Wingit

One day I went up to the field to feed my chickens. As I approached the run my heart sank. Blowing across the grass and plastered up against the wire netting were great drifts of feathers. 'Oh no,' I thought, 'we've had a visit from the pesky fox. When I open that chicken house it's going to be carnage in there.'

I approached with a heavy heart, took a deep breath and opened the door, expecting to see blood and feathers. Instead, all six hens strolled casually out and started to feed and scratch about. I was mystified and could not make sense of the scene.

It was not until about a week later that all fell into place. I was watching my birds again when suddenly one turned side on to me. Where she should have had a wing there was a ghastly black socket with thin bones protruding like sticks. Her wing had been pulled off. My birds had made themselves a dust bath in a dish-shaped hollow close to the wire, and the fox must have caught her by the wing through the fence. It didn't bear thinking about. She'd been left like it for a week.

I rang my sister Jean who keeps a lot of poultry and asked her what to do. She said, 'I wouldn't hesitate, I'd take her straight to the vet.' I thought, 'Yes, the poor thing has suffered all this week through my lack of observation, it's the least I can do.' I didn't have anything to put her in, so I took her in a picnic hamper.

In the vet's surgery there were a collection of people with dogs on leads, cats in those half-moon baskets, hamsters, gerbils, etc. I sat stony-faced because I didn't want anyone to ask me what I had in my basket. If they knew it was a chicken they might have thought I was a twerp.

Eventually I was called into the treatment room and I put the hamper on the vet's white table. 'It's a chicken,' I said. The vet's face assumed that deliberately blank expression people acquire when they fear they may be dealing with somebody unstable.

'I see,' he said.

I lifted her out and showed her to him. He exclaimed, 'Oh good Lord, what happened?'

I explained.

'Well,' he said, 'I'll do what I can.' He showed me the grim blackening flesh around the wound and went on, 'I'll amputate what's left of the wing and tidy her up a bit, but I'll have to give her a whiff of happy gas. Remember that birds don't cope too well with gas so you mustn't be too optimistic. Ring the surgery at about two and we'll let you know what happened.'

I went home with my empty picnic hamper. At about two o'clock I rang, and the receptionist sounded very buoyant. 'Your chicken's come round!' she told me. 'She's sitting up and taking a little wheat, you can come and pick her up.'

When I collected her, she was transformed, all smartly

stitched up with dissolving sutures and awash with purple antiseptic spray. The old girl looked alert and ready for action.

At home I hesitantly put her back with the other hens because the vet said they might peck and bully her. They didn't, she caused not a ripple. All six pottered off.

I was pleased about Wingit, as we all started to call her. Although it was a grisly story, it had a perverse kind of happy ending. The fox got some of her but not all, and she lived to lay another day.

The only thing I don't want you to ask me is how much money I had to pay the vet.

I am much too embarrassed to tell you.

Ode to a Jack Russell

Oh WHY must you bark at the postman?
Why must you batter my ears?
I know it seems rum
But the postman *has* come
Every morning for SEVENTEEN YEARS! *

* I hoped she might have got used to him by now ...

Inland Waterways

Now and then, as I toil along motorways or shoot through the countryside sealed in a packed train, I look out and catch a glimpse of a canal. Just for a second, I see a winding waterway of exactly the right width, and the pleasing curves of a little white bridge. There might be a lock-keeper's picturesque house, the garden bright with flowers, and massive black-and-white timber lock gates set in mown grass. Everywhere there would be smartly painted narrowboats moored companionably nose to tail, or bustling off to some enticing and beautiful waterway pub.

I always view these scenes with regret and a sense of loss. They seem to say, 'Look how lovely we are and yet you never come near us! You never even look twice!'

I want to protest: 'I do! I will! One day I'll get out of this stale, suffocating train and I'll sail down that cool green water. I'll slip under the darling bridge and those descending branches will envelop me. I'll be all by myself in the glorious silence and the only company will be swans and otters and coots. I'll be gone, just swallowed up into that mesmerising beauty, and vanished ...'

One day I finally had the chance of a holiday on the Kennet and Avon Canal. When I excitedly told my best friend, her response was meagre and dampening. She said she had boarded a narrowboat with her husband and two children for a similar holiday. They had set off in high spirits. After they had travelled slowly in the rain for the entire morning, the offspring became bored. Having raked over and consumed most of the food, they now squabbled and complained about the slowness of the journey. Husband and wife fell out. My friend called up a taxi on her mobile, got off at the next road bridge, and with a sharp 'Bugger this for a lark!' went home and left them to it. I was sure my own holiday would be serene and harmonious, but an unwelcome seed of doubt had been sown.

On the day of the trip, my husband and I turned up at the wharf in Devizes with a remarkable amount of baggage, two sons and a black dog. From the wharf shop we bought canal maps, information on waterways etiquette and pamphlets on the wildlife we might glimpse on our travels. I was startled to see goldfishes and terrapins listed. Apparently, people get fed up with keeping them as pets and dump them in the canal.

This is not a good idea.

Our narrowboat seemed very large and not in the first flush of youth. My husband had never skippered this or any other craft before. We were given a fairly perfunctory account of its workings, then set off in glorious sunshine. All seemed well until another boat appeared coming towards us. My husband blanched. He said, 'It's like driving a cricket pitch!' and as the approaching craft neared, he muttered through ashen lips: 'I hope that bloke knows how to avoid me because I sure as hell don't know how to avoid him!' A desperate silence descended on our vessel as the gap between us closed, and we steeled ourselves for the splintering of wood and cries of anguish. The two craft glided silently past each other.

In due course, a fragile confidence developed but this evaporated when we saw our first lock. Locks are very dark and frightening. One of your party goes, without conviction, to the lock mechanism and turns it the wrong way. After numerous failures, the great black doors yawn open and you sail forwards as if into a trap. The doors close. The water-level drops. You lose sight of the sunny banks and descend into the pit. Shaggy, streaming black walls loom over you like those of a tomb or foul dungeon. Curious faces peer down from the rim. For those onlookers you pathetically try to look seasoned and confident. The descent ceases and suddenly the black doors part, relief floods in and the sunlit waterway stretches ahead. The ordeal is over and you sail out and away. Until the next one.

Our dog Gemma came from a dogs' home. She was anxious to please but unsure about sailing. Mortified at the prospect of jumping on and off the boat, she only did so after much loud encouragement, and then in an eyes-shut 'Well if I must' fashion, which meant she usually fell in. We had to keep fishing her out. Nervous and looking for reassurance, she took to creeping alongside our beds in the dead of night, and upon finding any drooping human hands set about them with great wet slapping licks. People were galvanised with terror and sat bolt upright in the cramped cabins, cracking their heads and fearing a serpent had risen up from the silt.

I liked being on the canal but did not enjoy the cooking. The fresh air gave my family voracious appetites. No sooner had I produced one meal and washed up awkwardly in the miniature sink than they were enquiring about the next. It was blazingly hot and conditions in the tiny kitchen became stifling and ratty.

One evening I was cooking an intricate and complicated dish, a pan of sausages. There were too many for the small frying pan and they rose up the sides. I had to keep stirring them so that they all obtained a fleeting glimpse of the heat. It was boiling hot, poised above the spitting pan, but upon opening the little sliding window before me I was blinded by a cloud of mosquitoes which swarmed in, fangs first, looking for blood. On we sailed with the chef swearing and swatting. After that night we took to eating in pubs.

I also learned to do the narrowboat walk. The layout of many boats seems to consist of a long corridor up the right-hand side with the little rooms giving off to the left. Therefore the wall to your right becomes the curving ceiling over your head, and if you are tall and walk normally, you scrape your shoulder and pulverise your skull. This calls for the narrowboat walk, whereby from the feet to the pelvis the body faces forwards and from waist to neck it turns sideways, with the head turned to face forwards to see where you are going. It takes a bit of practice.

Certainly, the trip awakened my latent resourcefulness. Our son James celebrated his birthday on the second day out. Having forgotten to bring Sellotape, I fixed the jolly gift wrap around his presents with dental floss.

To make the birthday special, we had a secret plan. We would potter along the canal, not letting on that all had been set up in advance, and exclaim, 'Why, here's a cracking-looking village. Let's go and see if there's anywhere nice to eat!' Amazingly, we would then happen upon an exquisite thatched inn (previously picked from a waterway pub guide) and upon entering find a table set up with birthday balloons, cake, etc. It was a grand plan to fill any fond parent's heart with anticipation. The only trouble was the slowness of the boat.

The morning's leisurely pace quickened towards the afternoon. Conspiratorial smiles on parental faces froze as the hands of the clock spun. By teatime we were flat out at four miles an hour, the breeze stirring my husband's hair as he urged the great lumbering oaf of a boat forward. Consulting the map, we found we were still *miles* from the village. Panic set in. We rang the pub at seven, eight, nine o'clock to say we were running late, and only finally sprinted in, crazed with hunger, at ten o'clock. To the landlord's everlasting credit, even at that late hour the birthday supper was ready and welcoming. I learned that on the canals you have to allow *plenty* of time for your journey.

I Love a Little Narrowboat

I love a little narrowboat, I love the old canal,
Imagining those tales these ancient waterways could tell,
I love to work the locks, those oaken gates so firm and strong,
With know-alls up above to tell you what you're doing wrong.

I love to see the native creatures busy at the brink,
The otter and the water vole, the terrapin and mink,
And peering in the water, into shallows green and still,
To see somebody's goldfish from the kitchen windowsill.

I love to moor along the bank and hear the gentle rain,
To cook a meal and watch the world beyond the windowpane,
Little bobbing moorhen chicks, the mallard and the coot,
Exhausted lovers hoping that their effort's bearing fruit.

I love the ancient bridges, every keystone, every corbel,
The singing of the little birds, the chirrup and the warble,
To feed a lonely swan, so perfect, white as alabaster,
Who raised her wings and hissed, and so we sailed a little faster.

I love to meet the other folk who use the waterways,
The walkers and the fishermen on sunny languid days,
We drift beside the towpath and we breathe the summer's breath,
Till roaring motorbikers come and frighten us to death.

I love the inland waterways and if it's in my power,
I'll just keep on sailing at about three miles an hour,
And when I see that final tunnel, into it I'll glide,
I'll raise my yachting cap and see you on the other side.

Unfed Calf

We kept Dexter cattle for about ten years, the Jersey-sized ones, not the tinies, and this poem probably won't mean much unless you've kept cows yourself or had a lot to do with them. Steve Poole is a marvellous shepherd, stockman and friend; I called on him and his equally skilled wife Sally far too many times when I was at a loss. Steve had a way with cows, even crabby, kicking ones like Min. I still feel guilty about her. I let her get too fat, so that giving birth to her calf was harder than it should have been. She felt rotten afterwards and wasn't interested in her calf. He was cold and starving to death, having had neither the special rich colostrum so crucial to survival, nor his mum's great caressing licks. I was in despair but Steve, as always, came to the rescue.

When I read this, I am back in that stable holding my breath, willing Min to let the calf feed, not to kick him off, to leave the poor little guy alone.

Steve Poole stuck his fingers in the calf's mouth,
'If the suck reflex has gone,' he said, 'we've had it.'
I picked up the calf, heavy, a dead still weight,
and ran for the little stable and confining yard.
Min ran behind, gross untapped udder thumping from side to
    side,
Brown face frantic with concern, moaning with maternity,
The arch villain,
The bad mother.

Min, distracted by a bucket of nuts.
The calf is trundled forward, nose first, jammed in position with
    a knee at the back,
'Now then, Titch,' says Steve Poole, clasping the muzzle,
    'now then, get in there.'
Whack! A great ratty hoof swings forward,
Thwack! In the surprised face of the hungry calf
who retires defeated.
Perhaps not, then,
Perhaps I'll just stay hungry then.

Back in position. Careful transference of the hopeful sucking,
The ridged palate, from barren finger to fruitful teat.
Min munches the nuts.
We hold still and watch the calf,
See the sweet, beautiful undulations of the throat as it swallows,
The curve of the neck. The shock of interest.
At last a flow of relieving colostrum,
The lifesaver.

Good girl, Min, we rub her pin bones. Good girlie, Min.
New life for the calf, rejected and fading,
Now its hollow belly swells roundly out,
Fat with special recipe,
Primrose yellow,
Antibodies,
Anti-baddies,
Mum's magic.

I Was Standing by the Cow

I learned that although Dexter cattle are characterful and appealing, it's wise to be very careful around them because it is so frighteningly easy to get hurt. This is not so much because one of the animals takes a dislike to you, more that one further back in the huddle takes a dislike to her neighbour. She bunts the neighbour, the neighbour cannons into the one you're talking to, and you in turn are perfunctorily flattened …

I was standing by the cow, who was standing by the cow,
Who was standing by a cow who got annoyed,
For gentle summer zephyrs,
Had unsettled all the heifers,
And they ran around the pasture overjoyed.

But the cow by which I stood, wasn't feeling very good,
She was out of sorts and disinclined to play,
It was rather pitiful,
She had hoped to meet the bull,
But the blighter turned and walked the other way.

Well, it made the others laugh, but she
    hankered for a calf,
And would make a perfect mother she was sure,
A little calf, in sweet repose,
With a pink and shiny nose,
A version of herself in miniature.

Well, they had a bull named Floyd, he just stood
    there unemployed,
Or would feign a sudden interest in a star,

And the cow, whose name was Nancy,
Well, she didn't take his fancy,
So he walked off saying, 'La di da di dar.'

Nancy gave him such a bunt, struck him squarely in the front,
He was wearing an expression of surprise,
A domino effect resulted,
In that Floyd was catapulted,
And his whole life slowly passed before his eyes.

I was standing by the cow, who was standing by the cow,
Who was standing by the cow who got annoyed,
The flowers were sweet, the bees were humming,
And I never saw him coming,
I was flattened by a fat and flying Floyd.

So by way of chain reaction, I have both my legs in traction,
And I watch the daily setting of the sun,
So if the cow by which you labour,
Has a mind to bunt its neighbour,
Do not stand on ceremony – run!

The Animal Shelter at Gardners Lane

I am very pleased to be a patron of the Cheltenham Animal Shelter in Gardners Lane, Cheltenham. During every normal, non-Covid year, the shelter has an Open Day to raise funds, and the sun usually shines on the event. It's always a hugely happy day, thronged with dogs which were adopted from the shelter. In a joyous range of shapes and sizes they come along with their families, all looking much-loved and happy. Amid plenty of barking, there are classes, stalls and refreshments, and the overwhelming atmosphere is one of great kindness because all these wonderful people chose not to buy some expensive, fashionable breed of dog, but instead decided to come into the shelter, look round the hopeful faces and take one of our animals into their home and their heart.

I've always had a dog, and most of them were from shelters. Someone once shocked me by saying I must be very brave to take on a dog from a dogs' home. He thought they must be very fierce or flawed but that really isn't the case. So many dogs are admitted because of relationship break-ups, loss of the home or job, or the onset of illness. It's *always* worth checking the animal shelter first when looking for your perfect pet.

This is the poem I wrote about the animals waiting for a home in Cheltenham and every other animal shelter. I read it out at the Open Day. You couldn't hear a word I said because scores of dogs were all barking at the same time. They didn't think it scanned.

*

There are rabbits and guinea pigs, fancy and plain,
At the animal shelter in Gardners Lane,
Terriers eager to sniff out a rat,
Puppies who long for a cuddle and pat,
Older dogs, portly and easy to tire,
Who dream of a basket up close to the fire,
Gerbils and hamsters, downcast and forlorn,
And floppy-eared rabbits to nibble the lawn.

Beautiful creatures to suit every taste,
Lovable animals going to waste,
Cats of all colours, the modest, the vain,
Who had a home once and would like one again,
But family circumstance blows them off course,
Through bad luck or cruelty, death or divorce,
No longer required, left out in the rain,
They come to the shelter in Gardners Lane.

Here they are welcomed and vetted and fed,
With a kind friendly voice and a comforting bed,
And the breakfast's on time, and the brush and the comb,
And the walk in the grounds. But it isn't a *home*.
A place to belong; they would love it so much.
A basket, an armchair, a garden or hutch,
It's what they all dream of and hope to attain,
At the animal shelter in Gardners Lane.

So at night, when the darkness is studded with stars,
Please remember the faces that look through the bars.

A Dog at Home

I always like a dog at home,
It makes it nice and hairy,
And if a burglar calls,
Your dog will make the place sound scary.
Your dog will idolise you,
And his love will never stop,
You only need some food and drink,
A bucket and a mop.

The Seagull

There was an outcry in the Suffolk town of Aldeburgh when, in 2009, harsh penalties were introduced for feeding gulls. The hungry birds were perceived to be such a threat to public health and safety that a person tossing a chip, say, or the malodorous wreckage of a beefburger, became liable to a maximum fine of £2,500. I felt this to be unduly hard-hearted. £2,500 is a vast amount of money especially as, when it comes to feeding the seagulls, you don't always have a choice …

The seagull sits, like all his breed,
Pink of leg and bony-kneed,
Yellow eye prospecting hard,
For any tourist off his guard.

Down below, a pleasant scene,
A family, by the sea washed clean,
With fish and chips upon their laps,
Dad stands to take some family snaps.

Before his lens, a creature flies!
Father can't believe his eyes,
Enraged, he bellows, 'Oh my God!
A seagull's had me battered cod!'

A vile curse pollutes his lips,
'The b*****d's had me fish and chips!'
On high the bird, triumphant, sleek,
Smacks his vinegary beak.

Dog Pearly Gates
(A sketch)

I wrote this sketch for my BBC Radio 4 series *Ayres on the Air*. My friends Felicity Montagu and Geoffrey Whitehead made up the stellar cast, with me playing the 2nd Angel. I know how deeply soppy and sentimental it is, but it makes me cry. It's extraordinary because I *wrote* the thing, yet every time I read this it never fails. It makes me cry.

Maybe it's because so few dogs get a happy ending.

Cast: 1st Angel   Felicity
       2nd Angel   Pam
       Benjie, an old mongrel dog   Geoffrey

FELICITY and **PAM** are angels at the Pearly Gates.
FELICITY is playing a harp.

(Harp music suitable for the Pearly Gates)

PAM   Shhhhh! Stop playing that harp!

(Harp music stops)

FELICITY   Why? I'm supposed to play it, I'm an angel at the
            Pearly Gates.

PAM   I know, so am I, but someone's coming. Look, down
            the path.

FELICITY   Crikey, it's a dog. Are we expecting anybody? Have
            a look in the ledger.

PAM   Yes, here it is look. Benjie, elderly dog, road traffic
            accident, Tottenham Court Road, 3 p.m. this
            afternoon.

FELICITY   Poor animal. He looks all in. *(Calls)* Come on
            Benjie, not much further!

PAM Well done Benjie! Now you can have a nice sit down!

BENJIE Oh, I'm absolutely finished. What a long path! Where IS this place? What happened?

FELICITY *(Lightly)* What do you think happened, Benjie?

BENJIE Well I don't know, I found this ball. In the park. I was on my own, as usual, and I was just nosing it along. I suddenly realised I was on the road and then I looked up and saw a bus! I thought I was a gonner! COR! Look at those GATES! They're so white and shiny, somebody important must live here!

PAM Yes.

BENJIE But is it a good *home*? I've had enough of rubbish homes, tied up all day, just in everybody's way.

FELICITY Was your last home like that?

BENJIE After my master died it was. Real rubbish. I'd had such a nice master. I miss him every day. He used to wear a tweed hat you know, and he carried a stick. He used to do this special whistle just for me. They told me he'd died but I still looked for him. I searched for him every day, but I never found him.

… So is this a good home, would you say?

PAM   This is a really good home Benjie. You look through these gates. See all those fields and hedges? The nice wood and that lake for swimming?

BENJIE   Oh I love a dip. I could never get one down the Tottenham Court Road.

FELICITY   Well you can have as many as you like here.

BENJIE   And can I go and sniff *anywhere*?

PAM   Anywhere you fancy. On your own or with the other dogs. Now, you're tired, let's get you settled in. See those kennels on the left-hand side?

BENJIE   Yes, very plush …

FELICITY   Yours is the third one on the left, with the blue drinking bowl outside. There's a lovely clean bed and a bowl of your favourite, let me look in the ledger … Beefy Treats, is that right?

BENJIE   How did you know THAT? The third kennel on the left you say …

                   (Pause)

                   Who's that bloke standing by my kennel then?

PAM   What bloke is that?

BENJIE   *(Embarrassed)* Oh, stupid, for a minute there I thought … I thought it might have been my master … it's somebody wearing a tweed hat …

FELICITY   A tweed hat?

BENJIE   And … carrying a stick.

PAM   Perhaps you ought to go and investigate, Benjie …

BENJIE   He's doing my special whistle! I believe it IS my master! I think I must have died and gone to Heaven!

(Sound of scampering feet as he tears off)

FELICITY   *(Quietly)* Funny you should say that Benjie …

PAM   *(Quietly)* Could be *exactly* what you've done.

The Racehorse Fred

I gave this poem an enigmatic finish, so enigmatic in fact
that at the end of my performance I get accosted by anxious
people demanding to know what happened to Fred ...*

*

This is the final will and testament,
Of me, of Fred the horse,
For I am running in the National,
And I may not stay the course,
So of my wishes and intentions,
This will be the legal proof,
From me, the racehorse Fred,
Me being sound in mind and hoof.

Now I have not much to leave,
But, anxious to avoid the fate,
Should I fall at Becher's Brook,
Of therefore dying intestate,
I bequeath to my friend Bob,
The hay net, where I daily chomped,
And my rug, but he's a Shetland,
So he may be rather swamped.

Bob and I have stood together,
In the sunshine and the rain,
He will be the one to miss me,
If I don't come home again,
To my dear stable companion,
Who will be down in the dumps,
I leave my pack of Polos,
And my bag of sugar lumps.

For I was bred to race,
A thoroughbred is what I am,
From the time I was a foal,
Safe in the paddock with my dam,
My mother, such a mare,
Her velvet muzzle and her scent,
And our stallion was a champion,
But I never met the gent.

I see my jockey now,
I see with grins his face is plastered,
I see him flex his whip,
The little spiteful short-arsed b*****d,
For him, my lucky horseshoe,
He might like to bear in mind,
That I kicked it off at Chepstow,
And it hit the bloke behind.

I don't think people care,
About the *horse* that they have backed,
At twenty-five to one,
At Kempton Park or Pontefract,
It's the fortune won or squandered,
It's the shiver down the spine,
It's the flutter of the racing silks,
Across the finish line.

Now I canter to the start,
Imagining the final scene,
I may be greeted as a hero,
Or be down, behind a screen.
We are under starter's orders,
Blood, and labourer, and toff,
All are roaring in our ears,
It's death or glory boys …
    We're OFF!

* You needn't worry, Fred did get round. He came in a respectable third or fourth, and even as we speak is at stud in a sunlit meadow, eating daisies.

The Wildlife Garden

The wildlife in our garden,
It fills me with delight,
The sparrowhawk attacks by day,
The muntjac comes by night,
The fox is round the dustbins,
The rats they are not pretty,
The squirrel's on the peanuts,
And I'm moving to the city.*

* I was being outrageous here. I'm not moving to the city really.

The Terrifying Toaster

A few years ago we decided to plant a hedge, having decided that two smaller fields would be more useful than one big one. A hedge would be an attractive way to divide it, and unlike a barbed wire fence it would change with the seasons and provide homes for small creatures.

I had no idea what a lovely project this would be, how you could sit with a catalogue of hedging plants and put together

your own special mixture, like a recipe for a cake. It felt very self-indulgent. I chose holly for Christmas, hawthorn for creamy flowers and bird food, dog-roses for their delicate fragrance and hips, honeysuckle for the beautiful late-night perfume, spindle for its shapely berries in such a ludicrous shade of pink, sloes for making sloe gin and so on. All the little slips were planted like flimsy unpromising sticks and the whole thing was fenced in to deter rabbits.

Over the years, it thickened up. Unabashed by its wispy appearance, it shot skywards, all the various plants enmeshing and knitting together. From year one it was a delight. After its first proper cut this winter, it looks like the real thing. Still short in stature of course, but undeniably a proper hedge. Birds flit along its length, build their nests and sing with gusto. I walk beside it with my dogs on most days of the year and there is always something interesting to see.

We have two dogs of our own, and I often look after two more, belonging to our son and daughter-in-law. One is a beautiful black Labrador called Crumpet. At this particular time something had frightened her; she was nervous and lacked confidence. This was evidenced on walks by her wanting to keep me in sight at all times. One day we were sauntering along, and somehow Crumpet had finished up on the wrong side of the new hedge. This didn't matter because, as it was short, she could still see me over the top. Our other dog, the crabby but much-loved Jack Russell named Tats, was lame with a sore paw. The dew claw had snapped near the base, painfully exposing the quick. She was not enjoying the walk and limped along grim-faced, saying 'Me foot! Me foot! How much further?' She seemed worse than when we started out, so I made the mistake of kneeling down to inspect the poorly paw. Crumpet, on the other side of the hedge, suddenly couldn't see me. Gripped by anxiety, she took a short run, leapt up and sailed over the top.

Standing up from looking at the foot, my head was struck with enormous force by the unusual projectile of a hefty black Labrador. The impact was tremendous; I was knocked flat. Lying in the field, the sky and trees revolved around me in comic-book fashion. It was some time before I could get up and stagger home.

That afternoon I was going to a silver band concert, and especially looking forward to it because my niece, who plays the flugelhorn with great fluidity and beauty, was taking part. Once seated in the auditorium, however, I developed a powerful headache no flugelhorn could ease. It was dire; it throbbed like a drum. I realised this was the sort of scenario where any sensible person would go to a doctor, and I imagined the conversation I might have with him when I got there. 'Tell me Mrs Russell,' he would say, 'how did you sustain the head injury?' and I would reply, 'Oh, I was hit by a flying crumpet.'

Crumpet is also afraid of the toaster. This sounds hilarious but is in fact desperately sad to see. During the last tense, clicking moments before toast erupts

from the fiery depths, she quakes pitifully beneath
the table.

I wrote this for her as a consolation.

*

Our Labrador is nervous of the toaster,
When we use it, she is paralysed with fright,
And it doesn't make the slightest bit of difference,
Whether we use wholemeal, granary or white,
We used to hope she'd scare away intruders,
And bark at burglars, that would have been nice,
But no, *we* have to put our arms around *her*,
And say, 'Don't worry, only one more slice!'

Dreaming of Fresh Fields

I wrote this for Freshfields Donkey Village near
Buxton in Derbyshire, a charity which rescues ill-
treated and vulnerable donkeys. Children with special
needs come to stay and, as part of their visit, help to
look after the animals. Both donkeys and children
seem to appreciate the arrangement very much.

*

I would like to think there is a place for me,
With clean water to drink, and a shady tree,
Where someone cared if I had enough to eat,
And brushed my coat, and trimmed my feet.

I would like to be with other donkeys too,
With boys and girls to hug me, and love me true,
I would like to be with people who are kind,
Where, when I die, someone will notice,
    someone will mind.

The Paper Ears

Here lies a rabbit, this thick mark on the road,
Pink paper ears blown by the turbulence of passing traffic,
Picked by magpies, tugged by crows, shaded by buzzards,
A stain, with fragile ears,
Upright.

Yet this was a perfect creature, this rabbit,
This infester of banks, this thief of crops,
Twitcher of nose, liquid dark of eye,
Digger, hop-skip-and-jumper,
Flick of a white scut in the grass.

One rabbit, doe or buck,
Warm fur glossy from the polished burrow,
An adventurer, quick and fecund,
With pink babies deep in the dark earth,
Snug and intertwined.

'Such a pest, such vermin!
Plenty more where that came from!
It's a pity you can't still eat 'em!'
If people spoke their thoughts aloud,
This is what the paper ears would hear.

The Swifts

We downsized from our family home, after living there for twenty-eight years. It was a nice old house and there were many reasons why I was sad to leave it. One of the most poignant was that swifts returned every year to nest in the roof. Once their young had hatched, feeding commenced, with the parent birds swooping endlessly down to scuttle under some inhospitable-looking tile to attend to their brood.

I so miss those birds, those black daredevil squadrons sweeping joyfully round the angles of that old house on summer evenings, the joy of their wild screaming flight. I miss the feelings of relief and welcome when they arrived, and the sadness at their leaving when summer ended, knowing these tiny, featherlight, other-worldly little birds had to fly thousands of miles to follow the sun, and that every spring their numbers diminish, and fewer return.

I expect the swifts fly at our old house still, I hope so. I have never enquired after them. Some people don't like them and net their homes against them and I couldn't bear to know that, out of all the tiles on all the roofs in the whole world, they could no longer access the ones they called home.

The swifts are back!
They slice the air,
They're back! They're back!
From God knows where,
Navigating, mile on mile,
To the very roof,
To the very tile.

These Empty Skies

In our new home, I was delighted to find that house martins
were nesting beneath the eaves. For five lovely summers
they chattered, flashing back and forth, but this year, 2021,
I waited and watched the sky but there was nothing.
Heartbreakingly, none came back to our house at all.
I am pinning my hopes on next year.

*

These empty skies are killing me, this spring.
No swallows, swifts or martins, not a thing.
Vanished from the meadow and the wood,
Silent now. I guess they're gone for good.

Two Little Crumpets

Crumpet, our son's beautiful black Labrador, is gone now, and a young walnut tree marks her small grave. Like most Labradors she loved water; any abandoned, sludge-filled cattle trough would do …

*

Stinky-Time

I've found a private swimming pool,
It's called a cattle trough,
But every time I take a dip,
I seem to get told off!

The Bad Idea

I like to snap at wasps,
I find it quite diverting,
But this one's rather hot,
And now my face is hurting …

Tippy Tappy Feet

I always believed I was a big dog person, preferring a large, loping sort of dog to the little pipsqueak versions you see trotting along looking self-important. For years, I said I never fancied one of those, thanks.

Then my neighbours' two female Jack Russell terriers were rudely impregnated by a passing boy Jack Russell, who saw the chance of a lifetime and jumped over the wall to oblige. Sadly, all did not end well. Both pregnant mums were expecting just one puppy, and one died. Both mums were seething with maternal instinct and so the surviving puppy came to be shared, commuting between the two lactating mothers and becoming as fat as could be, a little tri-coloured ball sprouting four legs. She was irresistible, the sweetest little dog you ever saw, and at eight weeks of age she came to live in our house and was named Tatty. For the next twelve years she made us laugh, drove us nuts and enhanced our lives entirely.

But the loss. When she was so incapacitated with arthritis that she couldn't even stand, when the vet asked me in his kind voice:

'Can she go for a walk?' No.

'Can she sniff round, and do anything a dog likes to do?' No.

That awful decision which all dog owners must take, to arrange the kindly end of a much-loved life, and to endure the gash of grief which follows. The crippling loneliness, and in place of an ecstatic welcome, only silence.

*

The days are slowly passing since I found her still and prone,
Since I took her to the surgery, and came back on my own,
Now, as my key turns in the lock, the sound I miss the most of all,
Are the tippy tappy toenails, as they skidded down the hall.

There was something in the welcome, there was something in
    her style,
In the jingle of her collar and ecstatic doggy smile,
The tail that wagged so furious, the eyes that shone so bright,
It's the silence. It's the silence. It is blacker than the night.

And if I'd had a rotten day, if I was tired and spent,
If I had found indifference in every place I went,
Always at my journey's end, when I was flat and lonely,
That little dog convinced me I was someone's one and only.

Her things are still around me; I have left them all alone,
A little greasy collar, a yellow rubber bone,
A hairy tartan blanket in her basket on the floor,
From which she sprang to terrify all knockers at the door.

How grievous is the emptiness on entering the hall,
How disproportionate; so great a loss for one so small,
For the music it is missing, and my home is incomplete,
The music of her tippy tappy doggy dancing feet.

The Pyracantha Anthem

On a *Gardeners' World* television programme, I was enthusing about certain easy-to-grow plants which not only look spectacular but also benefit wildlife by providing pollen, nectar or berries. Pyracantha is one of my top favourites. *Please* plant one in your garden if you have the space, because they are such generous plants with beautiful creamy blossom, a feast of berries in flaming red, orange or yellow, and thick cover ideal for nesting. All your garden wildlife, seen and unseen, will thank you for your trouble.

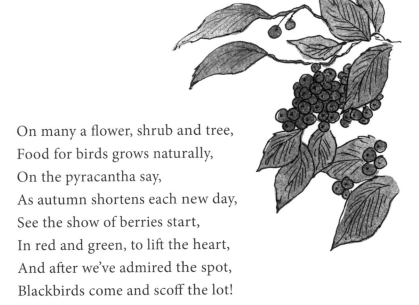

On many a flower, shrub and tree,
Food for birds grows naturally,
On the pyracantha say,
As autumn shortens each new day,
See the show of berries start,
In red and green, to lift the heart,
And after we've admired the spot,
Blackbirds come and scoff the lot!

Barking

This is about one of those homes monopolised by the family
dog. He is a perfectly nice animal, if a bit nondescript, but
every conversation is either interrupted by him, or revolves
about his various not-particularly-fascinating qualities. This
dog can do no wrong. His owner, believing you to be as
besotted as she is herself, makes a point of never talking
about anything else.

*

You made it! I so hoped you'd call in on your way to town!
Have you met our new dog, Charlie? He's a character, GET
    DOWN!
Yes, he's *very* spotty, you could take him for a leopard!
Breed? I think he's corgi, with a touch of German Shepherd.

In you come! I'll take your coat, sit down on that settee,
Oh, hold on just a second, I think Charlie needs a wee,
Out you go then Charlie! Do a wee-wee on the grass,
Oh no. It's more substantial. Mind your shoes when you go past.

Now, what can I get you? Tea or coffee? Vodka? Gin?
Oh, hold on just a minute, Charlie's barking to come in,
IN YOUR BED NOW CHARLIE! Oh, he wants to lick your hand!
He's always eating bird muck, *why*, I cannot understand.

IN YOUR BASKET CHARLIE! Stop that scratching! Where's
    your toy?
I worry over Charlie, he's a lovely little boy,
We got him from the dogs' home, I don't say he'd been abused,
But Charlie, Here! Fetch! Stay! Shake hands! You see? He seems
    confused.

Here's a cappuccino, chocolate sprinkled on the froth,
Biscuit? NOT YOU CHARLIE! Oh my God! I'll get a cloth,
It's gone all down your cardigan! It must have soaked right
    through!
Thank God it's just a shabby old worn-out one. Oh. It's new.

Oh no, how disappointing! Must you really go so soon?
I hoped you'd stay with me and Charlie all the afternoon,
Well, love to everyone at home ... be sure to close the gate ...
Be careful of your sandals round the ... obstacle.
    Too late.

Grinstead

The comedian Benny Hill was wildly popular in the seventies before his style of humour came to be considered distasteful and old-fashioned. He invented a rock group, The East Grinstead Syncopators, which I thought was hilarious. Finding myself in East Grinstead some decades later, I went into a toy shop and bought a puppet horse for one of my grandchildren. Jaw-droppingly, this non-event made the local paper: 'Pam Ayres buys puppet horse in East Grinstead toyshop!' raved the headline, and a journalist rang to ask if I had written a verse about the horse. I hadn't but I did. Here he is, viewing a racy scene being enacted in the stable yard:

*

I am Grinstead the puppet horse, I cannot walk or trot,
But from my shoebox stable, I'm observing quite a lot,
I see the shapely lady groom arriving with her dog,
The horses all get cuddles and the owner gets a snog.

Dosing the Dog

I was worried about my dog Ella. She had suddenly started to suffer from an itchy coat. All day long, underneath my desk, the dog scratched and fidgeted. I lathered her up with special shampoo from the vet, but nothing seemed to calm the condition. I asked my friends on Twitter if anyone had any suggestions, and many helpful replies flooded in. Had I tried tea tree oil? Or tea tree shampoo? Had I tried a product called Stronghold? Or garlic tablets?

I combed the internet and bought everything except the garlic tablets, thinking they sounded a bit unlikely. On researching the subject, however, it made more sense. Apparently, a dog which has eaten garlic gives off a slight smell, not noticeable to humans but highly repugnant to the microscopic parasites which burrow into the skin and cause irritation. Locating some tablets on the internet, I ordered a pot and within a few days the postman was walking up our path with it under his arm. I could smell him before he got to the door. The container was huge and looking at the recommended dosage I could see why. It said:

'Small dogs 2–5 tablets, medium dogs 5–10 tablets, large dogs 15–20 tablets.'

Ours is a large dog with a notoriously delicate digestion. That night, with her normal supper, I cautiously gave her just one garlic tablet.

Without wishing to sound tasteless, or to describe an unpleasant scene too fully, in the morning it was all I could do to get the dog out of the back door before there was the most tremendous canine explosion. I beheld the terrible spectacle unfolding on our lawn and the one thought uppermost in my mind was: 'Thank God I didn't give her the other nineteen.'

Over-Penguinisation

There once was an iceberg set in the cold seas,
And penguins lived on it, in twos and in threes,
The iceberg emitted occasional creaks,
And the penguins they waddled with smiles on
    their beaks.

But soon other penguins arrived at the rock,
Creating a vast, insupportable flock,
The food was exhausted, the filthy rock stank,
'Sod this for a lark!' said the iceberg,
    and sank.

159

Looking After Bees

I kept bees for a long time and finished up with ten colonies, but it isn't something to undertake lightly. The activity is immensely rewarding yes, but if you're going to do it properly you need to be aware of a lot of possible situations. The bees may swarm, which is their right and proper means of reproduction, where the old queen takes off with half the workforce, leaving the other half in the hive to look after various queen cells. The first new queen to hatch goes round and perfunctorily stings the others to death in their cells before they have a chance to emerge. This is brutal but it means that you now have one new, strong queen and a colony ready to rebuild.

Two viable colonies now exist. However, the old queen and her lot may not take up residence in a friendly hollow tree in some far-off wood. They may settle on your neighbour's drainpipe, and your neighbour will understandably want to know what you're going to do about it. You may have to shin up the drainpipe and retrieve them. You should invest in a good ladder.

You must also be aware of various problems which may afflict your bees and be ready with the knowledge and kit to tackle each one. A vile yellow tornado of wasps may appear and engulf your hive, overwhelming the bees, pinching every molecule of honey and leaving them to starve. The crab-like varroa mite is endemic; it bites and weakens bees. The much more visible mouse may take up residence, enjoying the warmth and thoughtfully provided honey, or you may have a catastrophic attack of hive beetle in which case your colony will collapse. For all these, and no doubt a host of newcomers, you must be armed and ready.

The equipment is bulky. There are many types of hive, all with assorted innards, and few from one type are interchangeable with another. You need the outfit, plus wellies and plastic gloves, and it is worth bearing in mind that as you will be mostly donning this stuff in the suffocating heat of midsummer while wreathed in smoke, you will assuredly reek.

Be prepared to lift colossal weights and cope with extreme stickiness when finally extracting honey. Getting it out of the combs, leaving aside honey from oilseed rape which sets rock-solid, is achieved by centrifugal force either powered by electricity or your own straining biceps in an ungainly barrel contraption called an extractor, which can either be expensively bought or hired.

The resulting crop must be bottled into spotless jars, and a label added bearing a best-before date and your address, so that the finger of blame may readily be pointed at you should a member of the public eat the product and be prostrated.

These are only some of the requisites. When I kept bees, I filled the entire shelved end of a good-sized barn with all the equipment I needed. These days, when I fancy honey, I tend to go out and buy a jar.

This unfortunate man is the husband of a keen beekeeper.

Stuck on You

I miss my lovely wife, she's gone, I've lost her, that's for sure,
Bees tampered with her brain; she is besotted, she's a bore,
She talks a different language, it's all gibberish to me,
With her Modified Commercial and her WBC.

She's working in the shed, I am a very lonely chap,
She's making up the frames and going tappy-tappy-tap.
I get no smile of greeting as she nails another batch,
Her mouth is full of gimpy pins. They might go down the hatch.

Every time I see my wife, I think I'm going to choke,
She's permanently trapped in an engulfing cloud of smoke,
We'd apples on the branches once, that how it used to be,
Now great swarms of honey bees are swinging from the tree.

I see a stealthy figure in the dingy undergrowth!
I catch a flash of metal and I swear a mighty oath,
'A terrorist!' I cry, and leap up brandishing the poker,
But no, it is my wife, complete with hive tool and a smoker.

My spouse was cool and fragrant, once we cuddled and we kissed,
Before she took the veil and called herself an apiarist,
She drops her suit and doesn't care what anybody thinks,
It may be smoke or sweatiness, but either way she stinks.

I miss her company, we don't do anything together,
She takes her bees to Scotland, they go camping in the heather,
Then when they come back again her one and only topic,
Is sunny Caledonia and honey thixotropic.

When buying birthday presents, I am overwhelmed with gloom,
She's not a gal contented with a bottle of perfume,
Her needs are very complex. Can I find, can I afford?
A solar wax extractor, straining tank and Snelgrove board?

Autumn is upon us, bleakly now the leaves are lost,
The hives protected from the cold regardless of the cost,
Varroa has been taken on with remedies assorted,
Mice are disappointed, Woody Woodpecker is thwarted.

My wife's on the extractor and the house looks like a slum,
She makes me wind the handle which in turn rotates the drum,
Thickly in the warming tank we watch the honey pour,
With hands stuck to the table and with feet stuck to the floor.

Now from our endeavour, see the product, see the fruits,
Of summer days spent sweltering in reeking gloves and boots,
By tanks of golden honey we are richly reimbursed,
I'd give my wife a cuddle … if she had a shower first.

A Moon Bear Song

I wrote 'A Moon Bear Song' at the request of the charity Animals Asia. These bears have a moon-shaped orange patch on their fronts, hence their name. Today countless bears are trapped in tiny cages and painfully drained of their bodily fluids. It is used in traditional Asian medicine.

A wind blows through the cages,
And a scent flows through the bars,
And the scent is of the forest,
And the mountains and the stars,
Of climbing on the roughened bark,
Of sweet air in the face,
Of kindly boughs to hold me,
In my leafy hiding place.

We are the little cubs,
We are the legless and the trapped,
For our clever body fluids,
We are punctured, we are tapped,
We are bundled into cages,
And the entries they are sealed,
And our shrieks cannot be heeded,
And our wounds cannot be healed.

We are in our tens of thousands,
We are countless and unseen,
We are hid in concrete prisons,
The infected and unclean,
We, the dwellers of the forest,
In our grim confinement must,
Grind the bitter bars,
Shattered teeth upon the rust.

But a wind of change is blowing,
And is rising to a roar,
For paws that fight the iron grille,
To feel the forest floor.
Through the courage of the farmers,
Through each thoughtful girl and boy,
Misery and pain
May change to liberty and joy.

Send a whisper to the suffering,
Each numbered nameless bear,
Lying spiked in iron cages,
In their anguish and despair,
That those who were my enemies,
May yet become my friends,
United for the animals,
Until the cruelty ends.

Puppies in Their Basket

It's weird, isn't it, how puppies all smell the same? It's a nice smell which disappears over time, and any puppies I've had the good fortune to cuddle all seem to have it.

There's been a dog in our home ever since I was fourteen. I'd spent the previous decade asking my parents if I could *please* have one which was like talking to a brick wall, so that when it was *Dad* who brought a dog home, that was an astonishing event indeed.

Dad worked for the Southern Electricity Board as a linesman, putting up and repairing electricity cables, and this took him to countless properties, some very remote. On one such isolated farm there was a puppy which took a shine to him and followed him everywhere. He didn't mention this at home at the time.

Some unspecified period later, he had to go back to the property where he found that the farmer was selling up. The now fully grown puppy was going to be destroyed, which Dad didn't like the sound of, and so he brought her home to our council house where there were already six children. Mother was tight lipped. To be honest, the dog was no looker. She was large, gangly, striped in a muddy-looking black and brown brindle and, unbeknown to us all, gestating twelve puppies.

She was our first dog and I've had one ever since, because they enhance life. Dogs force you to go out and stump about in the fresh air. They enable you to start conversations with

people without them thinking you're a weirdo. When you're down in the dumps they snuggle up beside you on the sofa, and are a true, loyal, understanding friend. It's a bargain though. At the front end of the experience, you have a puppy, a fragrant, floppy, needle-toothed, adorable charmer, and at the sadder far end, you have vets' bills, arthritic joints, noxious emissions, foul breath, and the dreadful heartbreak of parting.

I'd still choose owning a dog every time.

*

Puppies in their basket,
Smell as sweet as any roses.
Older doggies smell,
Of flatulence and halitosis.

The Dog Who Bit the Ball

I asked one of my little grandsons what he would like for his fifth birthday. 'A red football please,' came the quick reply. I was glad to have such a specific request. I wouldn't have to flounder through a host of other toys, not knowing what was any good. A red football, nice and simple. I set off to track one down, but it wasn't as straightforward as I thought. Sure, the shops had plenty of playful red balls, and an array of earnest-looking, proper brown footballs, but none of them combined the two requirements. In the end I went to a proper sports shop, with its peculiarly alien smell and ripped-looking assistants, and ordered one. There was a wait of several weeks before it arrived, but when it did I was delighted. A proper football, bright red as specified. Tenderly wrapping it up, I felt like A Good Granny.

On the big day I gave it to my grandson, and it was joyfully received. Just what he wanted! Hurrying out to the lawn, he carefully placed it and gave it an almighty kick. It soared through the air, closely followed by our Jack Russell terrier who leapt up, seized it, sank her teeth into it and gave it a good shake. All air was expelled from its innards. It rolled to a sorry halt, hollowed out and done for in the space of thirty seconds.

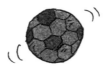

I am the dog who bit the ball,
And ruined the game of goals.
I wasn't to know, that balls don't go,
If you've added a couple of holes.
The kids and dad, they all went mad,
They sent me indoors, they did,
The ball was new, a beautiful blue,
And it cost them several quid.

The shame, the shame, I ruined the game.
And made the family crabby,
I jumped for it, I shook it a bit,
And it went from hard to flabby,
'Bad dog!' they said, 'Go in your bed!'
And in disgrace I go,
I offered a paw, but nobody saw,
Nobody wanted to know.

Here comes the boss, she's ever so cross,
Her face is black as thunder,
I'm in my bed, expression of dread,
My tail tucked down and under,
With hands on hips and scold on lips,
She tells me I'm a *menace*,
I'm finding it tough, this football stuff,
Anyone care for tennis?

The rule, you see, for dogs like me,
Is simple, I'll recite it:
Don't kick a ball for terriers small,
And think that they won't bite it.
I'm not too grand to lick her hand,
I sidle up and risk it ...
I think I've won ... look, everyone!
She's gone to get a biscuit!

The Curse of the Country Walk

What pillock hung the poo bag from the briar?
Leaving this unlovely scene,
Because,
If that's all you can do,
Hang up the doggy poo,
You might as well have left it where it was.

Worm Farm
(A song of the vermiculturist)

I was introduced to the notion of a worm farm by a friend in Robe, South Australia. We'd gone round to her house for a barbecue and she was keen to show off her new hobby. The contraption was parked outside the garage and looked like a stack of lime-green washing-up bowls on little legs. To call it a farm seemed a bit overblown. Whipping off the lid revealed layers of cabbage leaves and, er ... worms. It was interesting though, so when I arrived home I bought one of my own.

A worm farm produces a dark liquid and finely grained compost, both of which are unrecognisable from the original green waste. These products are highly nutritious to plants, and the process seems to me to be a good alternative to putting green waste into a licensed bin and carting it out on the street to be hauled away by lorry to a digester somewhere.

Admittedly, at first sight a large squirming ball of worms is a bit startling, but they are quite clean, pink and shiny. They munch up all the peelings I don't need, and since I bought my own worm farm I have decided they are a force for good.

I had a little worm farm, it caused a lot of rows,
It wasn't like a proper farm, it hadn't any cows,
We shredded up the cabbage, we were worm-farm cranks,
And we fed it to the worms, but they never said thanks.

A worm's disadvantage is, he won't do what you say,
He won't run and fetch a stick; he won't sit and stay,
He won't come to greet you with a bark and a bound,
Worms are rather limited, they just ... lie around.

We bought a proper home, with the bedding and the tap,
All delivered to the door by a worm-farm chap,
He gave us our instructions, all the things we had to do,
And promised us an avalanche of worm-farm poo.

Now worm-farm poo is a very special thing,
A heroic fertiliser: it'll nourish anything,
Benefit the garden and revitalise the pots,
So welcome, little wiggly worms!
    We hope you've got the trots.

A Failed Fisherwoman

My fishing career was brief and bloody. As a young girl I had gone with my big brother Tony to fish for trout along the River Ock which runs through our village. In a dark, still pool beneath the roots of an old willow, he hooked a rainbow trout in its beautiful spotted livery. My brother was ecstatic, and the fish was taken home, fried and eaten with lip-smacking pride. This all seemed fairly positive to me, so with impressive craftsmanship, I rigged up a fishing rod of my own out of a bamboo cane, a length of line, a hook and a quantity of bait formed out of bread moulded into small balls by my own grubby fingers. I set off heroically down to the Ock, at that time a little river brimming with life.

In due course I hooked a roach, a deep-bodied pretty fish with red fins. As soon as I took it out of the water, I was filled with panic at its suffering as it gasped and twisted in my hands. I had no clue how to take the barbed hook out of its bony throat. It had been second nature to my brother, but I'd never done it. As the fish struggled, I tugged and fiddled with the cruel hook, wishing I had never gone near the river. I got it out roughly somehow and put the roach, injured and despoiled, back into the river. Anxious for reassurance that it would have survived, I told my brother what had happened. He said, 'Well, if you pulled half the bloody thing's face off, you might as well have knocked it on the head.'

I never once went fishing after that, preferring to glimpse fish occasionally from a bank or a bridge, safe and happy in their own habitat.

Near where I live in Gloucestershire there are a lot of worked-out gravel pits which are popular with fishermen, and at various designated spots along the Thames other fishermen sit patiently under vast green umbrellas, sandwiches and flask at their side. Plus a dog. In rain or shine, but seemingly especially in rain, dogs of all shapes and sizes lie alongside their masters, all sharing the same look of boredom and resignation. If they had wristwatches, they'd be looking at them, sighing deeply and saying, 'Oh, for pity's sake, how much *longer*?'

The Fisherman's Dog

I wish my man would start to doubt,
The rectitude of catching trout,
And tire of these conditions dank,
Here, upon the riverbank.

I hope that soon he weary grows,
Of dewdrops dripping from his nose,
And, crouched beneath the brolly's dome,
Starts to think of going home.

I hope his flask runs out of tea,
I hope, for once, he'll notice me,
As my teeth chatter in my jaws,
And I am frozen to the paws.

Beside this cold and wintry stream,
Of my cosy bed I dream,
And hope my owner shortly may,
Give his fishing rod away.

But yet more fishes must he get,
To flounder in his landing net,
Another maggot hooked and white,
As onward, onward comes the night.

I'd love my supper in my bowl,
A blazing fire of logs and coal,
And in the firelight's homely glare,
To sleep with four feet in the air.

The Crackly Packet

In my experience, dogs are very good at choosing what they hear. Let's say it was cold and pouring with rain, and you invited our dog out into the garden for a late-night pee, well she might not hear that. Your voice might float unheeded over her sleeping form. On the other hand, if you picked up a crackly packet containing those dog treats that are supposed to clean their teeth, she'd hear that. Even if she were asleep in a distant part of the house with the TV blaring and somebody clog-dancing, she'd be up, ears pricked, and at your side like a shot.

I like the sound of a crackly packet,
Containing my favourite treat,
My human normally buys them,
From the shop at the end of our street,
They live in the crackly packet abode,
And my human's usual ploy,
Is to give me a treat from the crackly packet,
Whenever I've been a good boy.

When feeling the lack of a crackly packet,
You have to pull out all the stops,
Must be a good chap, jump up on her lap,
And give her a lick round the chops,
You can't declare war on a black Labrador,
When the thought of a tasty treat hits you,
You can't have a spat with the neighbouring cat,
Or jump on the back of a shih-tzu.

Humans are straightforward creatures,
They're partial to boxes of chocs,
And don't in the least like a carcase, deceased,
Or a roll in the poo of a fox ...
They fiddle about, with a kiss on the snout,
And affectionate cup of the muzzle,
They twiddle your ear, though you're making it clear,
That you only want something to guzzle.

Can't talk any more! She's just walked in the door ...
Her steely resolve, can I crack it?
I'm looking adoring ... devoted ... imploring,
Yessss! Here comes the crackly packet!

Dame Rose

On 19 April 2018, the five-year-old mare Dame Rose collapsed and died at Cheltenham Racecourse, having come fourth over a two-and-a-half-mile hurdle race. It was the hottest April day since 1949. She was one of six horses to die at the Cheltenham Festival that year.

*

Pray silence, pray silence, for poor Dame Rose,
Slip the sheepskin noseband down over her nose,
Lay a hand on her flank, she is down, she is done,
Dame Rose is dead in the Cheltenham sun.

Dame Rose was dainty and glossily dark,
Braided and booted and bright as a lark,
Two miles of endeavour and hurdles to clear,
On the hottest unmerciful day of the year.

Bring the tarpaulin now, put up the screen,
The mare Dame Rose is too sad to be seen,
The sweltering heat gave her much to endure,
But poor Dame Rose, she is cool now for sure.

Fruitless

I went to visit Mayfields Farm near Reepham in Norfolk, one of the farms owned by the Countryside Restoration Trust, a charity whose aim is to farm land productively while encouraging wildlife.

On that warm summer's day the place was stunningly beautiful, alive with hares and butterflies. I loved the hedgerows, which had been laid and then allowed to grow up tall, stockproof and heavy with natural food for our birds and mammals. Layer upon layer, the hedges were heavy with ripe fruit: blackberries, rosehips, hawthorn, sloes, nuts and crab apples, extending a welcoming feast for all, from tiny voles, which feed our owls, to fieldfares, arriving exhausted from as far away as Russia.

It makes good sense to me, allowing our hedgerows to bear their fruit. Some have to be cut for safe visibility on roads, but at a time when our wildlife is declining at a rate never before seen, I find it overwhelmingly sad that when autumn comes so many other hedges are bludgeoned, smashed to pieces and denuded of all their natural fruit.

How sad on this October day,
To see our hedges shorn away,
Small creatures would have liked to eat,
The hawthorn berries, rosehips sweet,
Blackberries and nuts and sloes,
But through the blades the banquet goes.
Please will someone heed our words,
And leave the berries for the birds.

My Sister's Cat Does Not Like Me

I hope that all readers like myself, to whom cats most
unjustly take a dislike, will be comforted when they read this.

My sister's cat does not like me,
See him, perched upon her knee,
How contented he appears,
As she strokes his velvet ears,
He purrs to her, his human mother,
Flexing this paw, then the other,
Saying to her 'I adore you,'
Say the word and I'll *die* for you.'

Yet when into the room step I,
The well of friendliness runs dry,
His eyes become as hard as flint,
And take on a satanic glint,
I have not harmed him, never once,
Yet he, with such indifference,
And dislike off the Richter scale,
Contemptuously flicks his tail.

If, ill-advised, I reach towards him,
To make friends and reassure him,
Be prepared for blood and gore,
And stand well back, for this is *war*!
His back is arched, his eyes are slits,
He hisses through his teeth and spits,
With rigid tail stuck in the air,
It's hatred, from the second stair.

I feel, when I am looking at,
My sister's most ferocious cat,
Relieved that I am not a vole,
Or mousy down a mousy-hole,
And though I know cats cannot shout,
I hear: 'Push off! Go home! GET OUT!'

My sister's cat's too hard a slog,
I'm going home to pat my dog.

Brown Hare

Suddenly everything had changed.

The vast stubble field, which all winter had been a haven of lush weeds and cosy hiding places, had been ploughed. In the course of just one day, machinery had come and changed the friendly land completely. Now there were only satellite-guided rows of bare earth, shining and dotted with gulls.

Ousted, bewildered, searching for the vanished familiar landscape, the brown hare ran along the side of the road, petrified by the passing traffic.

When I came back that way, she had been run over and was dead in the road. A thin river of crimson blood ran over the camber into the roadside dust. You'd have thought, wouldn't you, that she'd have been easy to see, easy to avoid, on that long, straight country road in broad daylight.

She wasn't long dead. I picked her up by the long back legs, which would no longer power her swiftly across the stubble. She was light, it had been a hungry winter after all. There was a bloody hole in her ribcage. I laid her down under the hedge so that vehicles would not ruin her any more.

I looked at her black-tipped ears, feeling gutted by this small loss, which is part of a larger loss, a monumental and awful loss of all of our fellow creatures. This beautiful brown hare would no longer lie flat on the bare earth to hide herself, would no longer make a form, a cosy nest for her cute leverets, which lie still and silent all day waiting for their mother to return to feed and warm them. Now she was just roadkill, pickings for magpies, crows and the big, pale buzzard.

When I walked back to my car, I looked up the slope of the field and clearly on the horizon was another hare, looking down at where its mate had been. It was in full view, watching, waiting for her to come back, so that they could spring away together, two of the swift, beautiful, other-worldly brown hares, which every year in our country grow fewer.

Leverets

We, silent and stilled,
Hid, hungry and chilled,
The night filled with danger and black,
Here must we lie,
And here must we die,
Our mother is not coming back.

Bamboo Toothbrush

I bought a bamboo toothbrush,
As I'd like to save the planet,
I bought it for each kittiwake,
and albatross, and gannet,
To try to send a message out,
To everyone like me,
Who always bought the plastic ones,
Which end up in the sea.

Fair Shares

I share my lawn with a couple of moles,
Share my carrots with a couple of voles,
Share my earth with a worm or nine,
Because the land is ours.
   Not mine.

I'd Rather Have a Sausage

Kuno, a four-year-old Belgian Malinois dog, was awarded the Dickin Medal for animal gallantry in November 2020. He was serving with British Forces and received gunshot wounds and life-changing injuries to his hind legs. Kuno was the first military working dog in the UK to be fitted with prosthetic limbs.

*

I won the Dickin Medal, see it here upon my chest,
Of all the brave heroic dogs, I was deemed the best,
Some dog-lovers ask themselves if it was humane,
Hearing of my injuries, my shattered paws and pain,
Other dogs admire me, telling tales of derring-do,
But I'd rather have a sausage.
    If it's all the same to you.

A Song of the Shires

Hook Norton is a village in the Cotswolds, famous for its much-loved traditional brewery and, in particular, for its fine horse-drawn brewers dray, a low and open cart adapted to carry barrels of beer. Beautiful Shire and Clydesdale horses trot round the local villages delivering beer to this day and are a familiar and much-anticipated sight.

This is a rollicking, sea-shanty sort of piece, as might be sung by … Shire horses.

*

If you're feeling flat and low, then to Hooky you must go,
A Cotswold village, picturesque and dear,
For there on certain days, you may see a brewers dray,
A spectacle to fill the heart with cheer,
Intimate or roomy, our pubs are never gloomy,
They are famous for their cosy atmosphere,
And a Clydesdale and a Shire (who have hooves instead of tyres),
Are furnishing the needy with the beer.

Furnishing the needy with the beer,
We are furnishing the needy with the beer,
People busy at their shopping,
Hear the clipping and the clopping,
When we're furnishing the needy with the beer.

It would be a sorry man, who exchanged us for a van,
Or a juggernaut which doesn't have a soul,
Heavy horses, smart and clean, have no need of gasoline,
Or diesel, electricity or coal,
Our only need is hay, just a couple of bales a day,
From the sunny Hooky meadows growing near,
And what we leave behind, gardeners are glad to find,
When we're furnishing the needy with the beer.

Furnishing the needy with the beer,
We are furnishing the needy with the beer,
Worry not, you Hooky drinkers!
We are coming, in our blinkers,
Furnishing the needy with the beer.

We hope you'll be impressed, when we're dressed up in our best,
And iron-shod on fine and feathered feet,
Going smartly at the trot: what a photo! What a shot!
Heading jingle-jangle down the street,
With noses pink and bristly, and nostrils white and whistly,
May Hooky horses never disappear,
While kegs are full to brimming, with splendour never dimming,
We'll be furnishing the needy with the beer.

Furnishing the needy with the beer,
Furnishing the needy with the beer,
While ale makes life look sunny,
And while you've got the money,
We'll be furnishing the needy with the beer.

Index of Animals in Their Groups

Birds

Cattle

Dogs

Equines

Insects

Rabbits & Hares

Fish/Sea Creatures

Other Species

Acknowledgements

Grateful thanks to Andrew Goodfellow, Michelle Warner and everyone involved with producing my book at Ebury; also to my wonderful literary agent Vivien Green of Sheil Land and my husband, Dudley Russell. Thank you all for your support, encouragement, friendship and good advice.